White Collar Prospecting

How to Replace *Random, Low-Percentage, High-Labor* Cold Prospecting with a Reliable, Trackable, Lead Generation Marketing Strategy

Shane Nichols

authorHOUSE·

AuthorHouse™
1663 Liberty Drive
Bloomington, IN 47403
www.authorhouse.com
Phone: 833-262-8899

Published by AuthorHouse   01/27/2025

ISBN: 979-8-8230-4061-7 (sc)
ISBN: 979-8-8230-4060-0 (e)

Library of Congress Control Number: 2024927126

Print information available on the last page.

Cover artwork by Arantxa Rosainz.

This book is printed on acid-free paper.

Contents

Part 1: Realize Your Biggest Challenge in Sales Today *Isn't Selling*

1   Discover Why You Need More Than Just Sales Training Today 1

2   What Sales Training Doesn't Teach You (That You Need to Learn) 6

3   How Your Employer Is Failing You as a Salesperson 11

Part 2: Why Cold Prospecting Is No Longer Effective and Worth Your Time

4   How Acting Like a Cat, and Not a Dog, Will Make You a Wealthier Salesperson 17

5   How to Fill Your Pipeline Full of Warm Prospects Ready for Your Follow-Up 24

6   How to Sell More by Working Less Hard 30

7   How Apple Makes It Easy for Prospects to Avoid You 34

8   The Biggest, Most Obvious, Yet Overlooked Secrets to Being a Successful Salesperson 39

Part 3: How to Get Appointments with Time-Starved, Hard-to-Reach Business Owners and Decision Makers

9 How I Took Control and Stopped Cold Calling 45

10 Whoever Can Spend the Most Money Attracting (and keeping) Clients ... Wins 56

11 How to Use Lead Magnets to Attract Prospective Clients 65

12 How I Built My First Lead Magnet 72

13 How I Built My Second Lead Magnet 81

14 How I Advertise My Lead Magnets 89

15 How to Win Over Other People's Clients 95

16 The Secret Weapon to Reach Business Owners 104

17 The 10 Habits of Highly Effective Emailing for B2B Sales Professionals 130

18 Using Your Own Media to Advertise Your Lead Magnets 150

19 Social Media—the Obligatory Chapter 156

20 The Persistent Salesperson's Way to Riches 170

21 My Results Generating Leads at Ball State Athletics from 2021 – 2025 180

Resources 219

About the Author 223

How I Can Help 225

Introduction

You are Good Enough at Sales, Get Better at This …

Why did I call this book *White Collar Prospecting*? Is it because I don't like, or respect blue-collar work? No, not at all. I grew up in Marion, Indiana. You could not grow up in a more blue-collar General Motors factory town. I've also worked my fair share of blue-collar jobs as a kid and young adult.

For most of my sales career I've had a blue-collar attitude towards prospecting. Acting like a bulldozer, endlessly cold calling and emailing prospects with a never-quit attitude, embracing rejection as a badge of honor.

But over the past decade I've noticed a trend. Cold prospecting doesn't work as well at is used to. And this shouldn't surprise anyone because times have simply changed.

About a century ago technology enabled salespeople to canvas neighborhoods door-to-door. It was the automobile that magnified their sales efforts and allowed them to cover larger territories more efficiently.

Then another technology came along, the telephone shifted selling from door-to-door to the more efficient over-the-phone.

Then technology changed selling again – TV and radio enabled sales messages to harness sight, sound and motion and moved selling from *one-on-one* to a more efficient *one-to-many* opportunity.

And now, once again, technology has changed selling.

Now it's the internet, email, smartphones, the shift to automation, and the growth in artificial intelligence.

Realize this: Prospects are busier than ever. They have more choices, and better information.

They have more salespeople calling on them than ever before. Most importantly, *prospects buy differently today than they did just 10 years ago.*

But for a variety of reasons, many sales organizations still cling to cold prospecting as their primary method to develop new business … ignoring the potential of technology … and marketing … while wasting the valuable time and energy of their salespeople.

Here's what I realized:

I'm good enough at sales.
You are probably good enough at selling too.
Most of us who've been selling our
entire lives have attained enough muscle
memory to be a competent closer.

Put me, or you, in a room with a good prospect, and we'll have a pretty good chance of closing that sale.

For most sales professionals, our lack of sales skills is largely *not* the problem.

The problem for most salespeople *today* is <u>getting the attention of our most desirable prospects</u>.

The real challenge is getting the opportunity to sell, **getting the appointment**.

One of my favorite movies (and books) of all time is *Moneyball* by Michael Lewis.

Billy Bean, the General Manager, had to rebuild his team (The Oakland A's) every season because big market teams (like the Yankees) could pay his players more money.

Billy's team was essentially a farm system for richer teams.

So, he decided to play a different game.

Billy became the first GM in professional sports to rely on data to select his players.

Prior to this, choosing who to draft, and pay millions to, was based entirely on human judgement.

In essence, evaluating talent was a crapshoot, done manually and prone to bias and severe misjudgment by the most experienced scouts.

But in the traditional world of baseball, this is how scouting had always been done ... and nobody thought there was anything wrong with it ... Until Billy Beane got tired of losing to the Yankees.

His data-based approach focused on a single stat that measured a player's contribution to winning:

On-Base Percentage.

More players on base = more runs scored = more wins. A similar metric exits in sales. In sales, it's **Getting Appointments with Good Prospects**.

More meetings = more presentations = more sales.

Billy's focus on OBP enabled him to find players who weren't on the radar of richer teams – meaning he could afford these players with his small-market budget.

His approach caused an uproar in the baseball establishment. Outrage, anger, disbelief, doubt, resentment – even from his own scouts and players. His own manager didn't even support him.

He risked losing his job, because early on, they didn't win.

But about midway through the season, things began to click.

The Oakland A's went on a record-setting 20-game win streak. That record stands to this day.

That year, Billy changed professional sports forever.

And in the world of sales, there is similar old-school mentality that still exists.

It's a reliance, and stubborn, sometimes nostalgic insistence on blue-collar cold prospecting.

When it has been clearly proven – and demonstrated – that technology and marketing can help in this process.

And to deny it, to not embrace it, to not study it, to not learn from it, is to act like one of those old baseball curmudgeons who refused to believe in data.

Another thing Billy says in the movie to one of his old-school scouts:

Adapt or die.

Darn right.

If you are in sales, and work for a sales organization who requires you to cold call and cold email prospects to find new business, this book is for you.

If you would like to learn how clever, low-cost marketing can turn you into a person who follows up with and attracts clients (rather than chasing them), read on.

To your success!

PART ONE

Realize Your Biggest Challenge in Sales Today *Isn't Selling*

In this section, I'm going to talk about the hardest task facing sales professionals today. It's not the actual selling part; I believe you are good enough at sales already. The tough part today is *getting in front of* a qualified prospect.

Getting appointments has become the most time-consuming and tedious task for salespeople today, and yet very little sales training or support is provided in this area.

Chapter One

Discover Why You Need More Than Just Sales Training Today

In my early twenties, as my sales career was just getting started, I decided to invest a considerable sum of money (that I didn't have) into sales training. Thank you, credit cards!

You might be wondering, *how much*? Well, it was about $10,000, a lot of money at the time – and is still a huge amount – but it was worth every penny. Why? Because I went from a guy *winging it* to someone with a **system**.

More on that later.

My first investment was in Dale Carnegie training, which I consider foundational sales training anyone can benefit from. If you don't know who Dale Carnegie is, he was a public speaker, lecturer, and aspiring actor.

While broke and living in New York City in the early 1900s, Carnegie began teaching public speaking at the local YMCA. His courses became a hit and spread to major cities across the country, and he went on to write several books.

His most popular was ***How to Win Friends and Influence People***, and this book continues to sell well today. I strongly encourage you to pick up a copy.

Dale Carnegie Sales Training teaches the fundamentals of salesmanship, like:

- Being polite and complimentary.
- Dressing professionally.
- Never talking too much.
- Having a genuine interest in your prospects and their lives.
- Asking good questions.
- Making people like you – and in return – more willing to buy from you.

In a nutshell, it's a reminder you can catch more bees with honey than vinegar. And I consider it my undergraduate degree in sales.

But my graduate degree came from the Sandler Sales Training program, which I consider the highest level of organized professional sales training available in the U.S.

In 1966, David Sandler found himself out of work and forced to go into sales, having never sold anything in his life up to this point. And it showed because, on his first 87 calls, he didn't sell a darn thing.

Sandler became frustrated with the sales training available at the time, all preaching blind enthusiasm and high-pressure, overused sales gimmicks like *The Ben Franklin Close.*

He teamed up with a clinical psychologist and designed a program that broke the traditional stereotypes of salespeople. He began teaching students to ***not act*** like other salespeople, to not represent the enthusiastic, eager image of what everyone pictures in their minds when they think of a salesperson.

Why? More than anything, psychologically, he found that acting like a typical eager salesperson summons the defenses of your prospects, putting them on guard, making it harder to gain trust and gather information necessary to qualify and complete a sale.

Sandler training points out that most of us are too concerned about getting approval from our prospects, clouding our judgment, and making it easier to give up on a sale, for fear of making our prospects angry or uncomfortable.

Sandler teaches that prospects are not your friends. Rather, *all prospects lie to you in one way or another.* Have you ever heard some version of these common objections?

"We've already spent our budget."

That's a lie. If they really wanted or needed your product or service, they would find the money.

*"It's too expensive; your competitors are cheaper.
Can you come down on price?"*

Almost always a lie and a brazen attempt to get you to lower your price – don't!

"Thanks for your proposal and presentation; let me think it over for a few weeks."

In the world of Sandler, just educated your prospect for free, and as a reward, they fed you another lie! I realized lying is commonplace in the selling process and most of us eagerly accept what our clients say as fact. Granted, these are mostly harmless lies – only if you consider *not* making a sale, hitting your goals, and maximizing your earnings as harmless!

This kind of legal manipulation only exists in a few other professions; like professional sports and the law. Imagine, in a football game, before hiking the ball, your quarterback yells out *the actual play* instead of the code normally used to confuse an opposing team's defense.

Imagine if you were accused of a crime and your lawyer **agreed with the prosecution** instead of presenting a favorable legal argument on your behalf to a jury.

In sports, in law, and in sales, manipulation is part of the game. It's allowed. It's expected. And if you accept everything a prospect says as fact, you'll end up wasting a lot of time and energy on the *wrong people* and earn A LOT less money. This was eye-opening for me because I inherently believed it was rude to upset a prospect, no matter how much *they abused my time and lied to me.* It all stems from programming from our childhood. Our parents teach us as children to be polite to all grown-ups. And it can be hard ... but necessary ... to adopt a more calculating *selling behavior* to maximize your time and effort.

You're not being rude when realize someone is wasting

your time, and not worth your effort, and you quickly decide to move on. It's just business. After all, this is not retail, we don't have to work with everyone who walks into our shop. In B2B sales, not everyone will be a good fit. Not everyone can walk into our store and be worth or time and effort.

This psychological insight is why Sandler's training (in my opinion) sets itself apart from any other formal training program.

And because of my investment in sales training, I've made a nice living for more than three decades. I am an expert qualifier and know where and how to spend my time productively. I know how to make clients comfortable, how to gain their trust, what psychological triggers are important, and how to create proposals and presentations that close.

This is what most sales training teaches you – some are better than others. But what you will find very little training or guidance on is this:

Getting the opportunity to sell in the first place!

That's right. Today, for a variety of reasons, it has clearly become more difficult *to get an appointment* with a good prospect <u>than it is to sell them something</u>!

And in my view, nobody is teaching salespeople the necessary **marketing skills** required to get appointments successfully and repeatedly with time-starved, overwhelmed dream prospects – including most employers.

Chapter Two

What Sales Training Doesn't Teach You (That You Need to Learn)

My point here is not to sell you on sales training. I recommend Sandler and Dale Carnegie no matter what age you are. Even if you don't have the money, when you invest in yourself, somehow it magically pays for itself. The year after completing Sandler training, I more than doubled my income, allowing me to pay off all my debt for the first time in my life.

Whenever I'm around other salespeople who haven't invested in training, I feel like I'm on another level, because I have a process to follow. I know I can sell circles around them.

One of David Sandler's famous quotes was:

"If you don't have a selling system of your own, when you are with a prospect, you will unknowingly default to the prospect's system."

But as good as those training programs were at teaching me to sell, neither one taught me how to **reliably** land appointments with increasingly time-starved business owners. And that in my opinion, is the greater challenge today. *Getting the appointment* or getting the selling opportunity.

Just as we as consumers today have more choices in almost everything we consume – from streaming TV services to types of milk – business owners today are similarly more distracted and overwhelmed than ever.

And a host of factors, like advances in technology, increased competition, shifting generational buying habits, are all contributing to our growing marketing challenge.

There are also unprecedented levels of venture capital and private equity (cash) funding more start-ups than ever and fueling massive consolidation in corporate America.

This means there are more salespeople calling on fewer buyers than ever before in the history of our country.

And it took me a while to realize this, but it now takes more effort to *get an appointment* than it does to sell *something!*

Just 20 years ago, a simple phone call or dropping by a business would land you some time with a decision maker. Then email became **the thing**, and now everyone has spam filters and smartphones that can block your calls.

For a few years, I had an enlightening experience that will forever change how I approach prospects. I was put in charge of buying millions of dollars of TV, radio, print, and digital advertising for a large ad agency in Dallas. After selling during my entire career, I finally got to sit on the other side of the table **and buy!**

I personally experienced the overwhelming sensation of having dozens of salespeople calling on me every day. I got to see firsthand how little effort most salespeople put into getting an appointment (and in my previous selling roles, I was no different).

Most salespeople made no effort beyond sending one or two emails. Many would call out of the blue, when it was convenient for them, and if I ignored the call, they'd leave a voicemail. If I didn't return their calls, some would leave a voicemail, but most would give up on the 2nd or 3rd try. 99% of the people calling on me *offered no compelling reason to meet with them.* The most common reason proposed for taking my time as a buyer: **They were selling something, and I had money!**

When I didn't respond to their first call, typically the next step was to call again (or email) with an increasingly angry tone.

Understand this: It's not a buyer's duty to meet with every salesperson who requests a meeting (unless you are lucky to be in an industry with very little competition – by all means, work for a monopoly if you can).

Chances are, you're one of a dozen (or more) different people vying for the attention of your prospect – each day.

The handful of salespeople who got my attention all had a compelling hook, angle, or referral; (more on these hooks and angles in Part Three of this book).

Think about it, there are really two steps to making a sale today, and *the first one isn't selling*:

Step 1: Getting a prospect's attention and getting the appointment.
Step 2: What you do in front of a prospect, the actual selling part.

And if you do think about it, which is harder? How much grinding and chasing does it take to get a prospect's attention these days? How many cold calls and emails does it take? How many times have you been rejected, and felt defeated, even embarrassed, or discouraged and frustrated? How many times have you doubted the possibility of hitting your goals? Or when you hit your goal, you immediately worry about how you're going to do it next year?

Prospecting has become joyless, repetitive, *tedious labor* unless you are a telemarketer and choose this line of work.

Most salespeople don't sign up for this. <u>Selling is hard enough without this extra work.</u>

So, consider breaking the sales process into two parts: The first is *developing a lead*, and that effort should be considered **marketing,** not selling.

And I will prove to you that <u>salespeople shouldn't be tasked with this effort</u> in addition to the actual selling part.

The second stage – nurturing a prospect toward a sale – **this part is selling**.

Most salespeople can handle the selling part!

Put <u>anyone with some selling experience</u> in a room with a client who's agreed to meet them, and they have a good chance of closing a sale. I'd say you have a 50% or better chance. And if you are one of those sales professionals who invested in sales training, I'd bet you will have a much higher close ratio (75% or more).

That is not to say the effort to close the sale will be easy. This is where good salespeople earn their money; they know how to close. Can you imagine a world where you could focus solely on meeting and closing **leads**? And take the *marketing* part – begging for appointments – off your plate?

Well then, now you might be onto something. Read on!

Chapter Three

How Your Employer Is Failing You as a Salesperson

Do you know the difference between a *lead* and a *prospect*? Let me first define what a *lead* is because most of employers confuse the two.

When I first started in sales, I had to build my own book of business, and the only way of doing it back then was by cold calling or canvassing. Email wasn't an option yet, and yes, I am that old!

Every now and then, because I worked for the local newspaper, and popular radio and TV stations, a sales manager would give me a <u>lead</u>, which I define as:

Someone who reached out and expressed interest in learning more about buying my product or service.

A <u>prospect</u>, on the other hand, has not volunteered any interest. They may be someone I *should* call on, but it will require more work.

Compared to following up with an actual lead, the difference in effort is night and day.

And the two should never be confused. Today, for many B2B sellers, getting *actual leads* from an employer is very rare. And that is in part, why I am writing this book.

Sometimes my employer and I agree on who's a good prospect, and sometimes not. For example, your boss may believe that someone doing business with your direct competitor is a *good lead*. True, they may be a **qualified candidate**, but they're not technically a *lead*. Because you – the sales professional – will still have to:

1. Spend considerable effort getting their attention and then getting them to meet with you.
2. Then sell them something.

If your employer gives you an actual **lead**, you are obligated to follow up. If they give you a **prospect**, you're only obligated *if you feel it's worth your time and energy*.

It's important to understand the difference between leads and prospects because the act of converting prospects into leads today requires a different kind of effort. It now requires a *marketing effort*.

Converting leads into sales: This is true *selling*.

Converting prospects into leads: This is *marketing*.

Just look around at the most successful and

forward-looking sales organizations – they separate the two functions.

They recognize that <u>getting consideration</u> from qualified prospects is different from <u>selling</u> to those prospects.

Salesforce, one of the most successful software companies in the world, credits their success to this very notion. And their salespeople, who they call Account Executives, make zero cold calls.

Their Account Executives waste ZERO time (and precious energy) on prospecting (the marketing part).

Instead, they assign a separate team – *a sales development team* – to do the marketing part, and this (to some extent) is why they continue to grow and how they consistently attract and keep great talent.

Problem is, most companies out there aren't equipped, ready, or willing to invest in this type of *lead generation marketing*.

I know this because I've exclusively worked for these types of companies and have many friends and associates in the same boat. It's too bad because ignoring the importance of marketing in the sales process today will eventually lead to one or all the following:

1. Stalled growth.
2. Higher employee turnover.
3. Higher client turnover.
4. An inability to attract young, and in general, top talent.

The good news is **you can do something about it** – just

like me – because you can learn how to position yourself to *attract* the right prospects rather than just *chase* them.

And if you develop the ability to attract clients, you will change your world – forever. You will go from getting rejected to **rejecting** *unqualified prospects* not worth your time.

Feel free to skip ahead to **Part Three** and start learning some marketing techniques that have transformed how I sell today. Or, read on to **Part Two**, where I <u>prove</u> to you that cold outreach is no longer an effective business development strategy or worth your valuable time and energy.

PART TWO

Why Cold Prospecting Is No Longer Effective and Worth Your Time

If you work in sales or employ salespeople and have no marketing in place to help generate leads, then you will be forced to cold call and cold email strangers.

In this section, I hope to convince you that cold outreach is, in fact, a waste of your time. And there are **five good reasons for this**, which are covered in the following chapters.

Chapter Four

How Acting Like a Cat, and Not a Dog, Will Make You a Wealthier Salesperson

The following story is told from a male perspective, I mean no offense to the ladies.

Imagine being out one evening with friends, and out of nowhere, a stunningly beautiful woman walks up and compliments you on your shirt, which features the logo from your favorite NFL team – she's a fan too.

The two of you go on to talk about your favorite team and find out you have other shared interests, and eventually it leads to getting her phone number AND a future date.

How much easier was this interaction because **she** opened the conversation?

It was 100% easier.

Night and day.

One of the most popular dating apps in the world,

Bumble®, is based on this very feature. In their app, the girl opens the conversation instead of the guy.

Now, let's flip the script.

Suppose you approach this same beautiful woman, whom you have never met, someone with no shortage of male suitors. In fact, before you summoned the courage to walk over and speak to her, 3 *other men* tried to hit on her.

What could you say to her to get her attention? And how likely will your cold advance lead to any meaningful conversation and the chance of getting her phone number?

In the first scenario, when she came up to you, she gave you permission to enter her world; she recognized you might be able to *add value* to her life.

In the second scenario, when you approached her cold, your position was lowered to that of every other strange man who's approached her in a social situation – often with cheesy one-liners. Even if a cheesy one-liner isn't your plan, you're still starting from a low position – AND it takes hard, persistent work to climb out.

This same dynamic works in selling, too. If you can get a prospective client to approach you first (in some way), it puts you in a much better position to make a sale. You'll be more relaxed, confident, and most importantly: *Positioned as someone who can potentially solve their problem.*

But when you call a prospect cold, even if they're familiar with your company, you trigger something psychological. People naturally run from whatever is chasing them. But they *respect*, even pursue, what is not easily obtainable.

This pretty much sums up why cats are a favorite house pet.

Dogs are obedient (mostly) and loyal, and they love to chase things.

Cats are indifferent, wayward, unruly, and masters of elevating their position through displays of agility and cuteness.

Dogs love you (and everyone else) unconditionally and will follow you anywhere.

Cats, on the other hand, do what THEY want, when THEY want, including going to the bathroom indoors!

And a cat's disinterest (and disobedience) is usually a source of pride among its owners!

In the world of sales, you want to be more like a cat – that is, if you truly value your time and want to maximize your earning potential.

Even if you represent the single best possible solution to your prospect's pain and problems, if all you do is *chase* them, you will always be stuck in this lower position.

And I'm not saying that's a bad thing; I've been that person for over 20 years now, chasing and then trying to prove myself worthy of a prospect's time. It's just a harder way of doing business.

Here's a fact: Good business prospects are a lot like beautiful women. They are in high demand and get A LOT of attention.

Pretty women, especially very attractive women, are chased around more than any other species on this planet, every day, all day.

From the moment they leave their house, *men notice, men smile*, and some men even stare.

And every day, sometimes multiple times each day, men will say things like *"You're soooooo beautiful."* And the first thousand times she heard this, I'll bet you she genuinely appreciated the attention.

Now it's just another day at the office.

Similarly, imagine yourself the beleaguered decision maker assailed by salespeople every day, who are all saying pretty much the same thing – fielding a constant stream of sales jargon.

Sure, most business owners have a begrudging respect for us salespeople; they know we're just trying to do our job. They realize nothing gets done in this world until a sale is made.

But when salespeople make no effort beyond cold-calling or cold-emailing at random moments during the day, offering zero value to their prospects, it gives your prospects the right to ignore you.

Men who break through with truly attractive women distinguish themselves from the chasers (dogs) by disrupting the expected pattern. They display their value socially or through indifference (like a cat). Some use humor, bravado, magic, whatever it takes to lower the defenses of their in-demand romantic interest.

You can apply this same thinking to how you approach business prospects. And thankfully, getting the attention of a time-starved business owner isn't quite as hard as winning the heart of a beautiful woman.

But to do it successfully and consistently requires extra

effort and commitment. And that is what this book is all about, making a creative and strategic effort, elevating your position beyond the typical salesperson, as someone who can add value to your prospect's world.

One proven way to attract clients is through *marketing*. Clients will show indirect interest in your product or service and download a report or white paper, or take your quiz, attend your seminar, or see your demo. This type of *published* information is a display of value, it's a display of expertise.

Like wearing the logo of your favorite football team might strike up a conversation with an attractive woman, these targeted displays of value demonstration can strike up interest in your product or service.

Heck, sending a simple letter (in the mail) before calling a prospect will set you apart from almost every one of your competitors.

Marketing will help you find clients with less labor than cold calling, and more importantly, *marketing will change how you are perceived* – by elevating your position as *a value provider* rather than just another pesky salesperson.

You go from calling cold to *following up* on **their** request, then delivering something of value.

This makes a HUGE difference. And that's really what this book is all about – choosing the benefits of *being someone who follows up vs. interrupting strangers.*

Move away from the chill, *and step into the sunlight.* Because *following up* is so much easier.

My favorite author on marketing and sales, Dan

Kennedy, calls this **going from an annoying pest to an invited guest.**

You might be thinking, *Sure, this works in business but back to women. How can I get a beautiful woman to approach me?* Try becoming a famous movie star; do you think Brad Pitt has any trouble attracting women?

Becoming famous also works in business, and it's easier to establish a name for yourself in your business niche or community.

You can join the Chamber of Commerce or the Rotary Club, run for office, speak publicly, host events and parties, write your own book, start a podcast, or radio show, host your own online TV show. You could also write a column for your trade publication.

These displays of value will help create a name for yourself as a value provider and you will begin organically attracting clients.

There is a higher level of business fame, like the entrepreneurs (salespeople) on TV, who get covered in the press. They publish *New York Times* Best Sellers, write columns for business and trade publications, have popular podcasts, and cultivate large followings on social media. Some travel frequently, speaking at seminars and other events. And as a result, these famous businesspeople have little trouble attracting clients into their world.

If you make the decision to spend your time positioning yourself through marketing instead of cold outreach, you can forever end the drudgery and labor of prospecting. You will make more money. And you will learn a skill that will help you for the rest of your life.

You will feel energized and in control instead of wondering where the next sale will come from.

And the greatest reward is the time and energy you can now devote to delighting and upselling your existing clients and warm leads.

Chapter Five

How to Fill Your Pipeline Full of Warm Prospects Ready for Your Follow-Up

Here is another quote from my favorite author Dan Kennedy:

"Any idiot can sell things to the ready-to-leap-now buyers, so it usually pays poorly and can even be a path to bankruptcy despite success at it. The wealth is in the (management, development, and ultimate monetization of the) not-yet-ready buyers."

<u>The most important reason</u> to NOT spend your time cold calling prospects is because 99% of them aren't ready to buy anything (or meet with you) in the moment you decide to call them.

Think about that for a minute.

Cold outreach, whether by phone or email, has become an almost pointless effort to convince a stranger to make a big decision, on the spot, like talking or meeting with you, before they even know who you are.

You can expect about a 1% success rate with this approach today.

So, for every 100 calls you make, expect 1 appointment. Not a sale, *just an opportunity to sell*. Those odds are almost as bad as trying to win the lottery.

Before the pandemic, my Sandler Sales Training coach, Matt Nettleton, hired an inside salesperson to make over 2,000 cold calls to his prospect list. This took her around 3 months. They ended up converting about 1% into appointments.

Mind you, this was under the supervision of a *sales training expert*, **using proven scripts and tactics, and not even he could do better than 1%!**

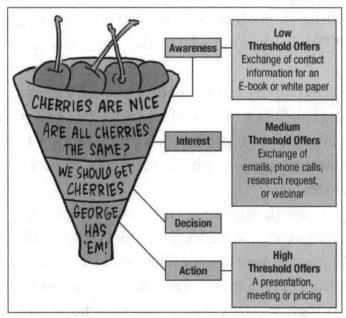

As prospects move through the various stages of interest, they are open to different ways of communicating with salespeople.

I would describe cold outreach as a very *high-threshold* way of interacting with prospects.

It assumes these important milestones are in place:

1. A client is interested in your product or service.
2. They have all the information they need to decide.
3. They trust you as a reliable source.
4. They are ready to meet you.

Only a small percentage of people fit these criteria on any given day. And depending on a variety of factors like what you sell, what market you operate in, how good your product or service is … you can safely assume 1% of your prospect pool will agree to meet with you and buy your product or service on any given day.

So, relying on cold outreach alone means you're wasting time sifting through non-buyers while failing to give the other 99% any ways to move further along in their buying journey.

A better approach, one used by the most cutting-edge sales organizations, is to offer *lower-threshold* ways of interacting with your product or service. The key to selling in the internet age is to give buyers more control over the sales process.

If you provide additional pathways to engage with your product or service, and enable prospects to learn on their own, you will position yourself as a value provider while attracting a larger pool of potential clients into your pipeline.

Now, back to Matt, the Sandler sales trainer. He offers

a variety of bridges appealing to buyers in every stage of the buying process for sales training.

Here are some examples:

Low-Threshold Offers

Matt advertises free educational information like books, guides, and research reports to those who want to learn more about Sandler sales training but aren't ready to engage with a salesperson yet.

These not-ready buyers may be willing to provide an email address in exchange for helpful information, becoming qualified leads for follow-up.

This effort of providing something educational, then following up rather than approaching cold, positions Matt differently – it positions him as an authority, not just another salesperson, but a trusted provider of helpful information.

Medium-Threshold Offers

Matt also conducts free seminars to attract those further along in their buying journey. This group is willing to experience a higher level of commitment and passively engage with a salesperson.

This alternative bridge gives Matt a great opportunity to convert warmer prospects into buyers by displaying his expertise in-person and further establishing authority.

High-Threshold Offers

Matt also conducts one-day paid seminars, or boot camps. These appeal to the ready-to-buy-now-prospects because there's a cost, and time commitment, and much like committing to an appointment or demonstration.

It's also likely most of the prospects committing to Matt's bootcamps also engaged with his lower-threshold educational offerings first.

In Part Three, I will dive deeper into how you can use these same tactics to attract more prospective clients. For now, just try grasping the benefits of giving buyers lower threshold ways of interacting with your products and services in addition to a meeting or consultation.

SOCIAL SELLING MADE EASY

Struggling with using LinkedIn to generate new business?

Sandler and LinkedIn teamed up for this joint book publication, *LinkedIn the Sandler Way*. Experts from the world's largest sales training organization and the world's largest networking organization share their insights.

Get this FREE 68-page e-book and learn the secrets to leveraging the world's largest online professional network to find prospects and increase your sales. A must-have book for any sales professional who wants to maximize his or her prospecting efforts using LinkedIn.

Find out more about this ground-breaking book! ❯

An example of a low threshold offers to download information in exchange for providing contact information.

Hi Shane,

Who do you know that should be sitting next to you in class? **Bring them to the October 30th Overview Class**. https://www.eventbrite.com/e/sandler-training-sneak-peek-tickets-50557639260

Tuesday Sandler Foundations - 8 am-9:30 am- Goal Setting with a Scorecard- Everybody sets goals but they seem so hard to achieve. More than 50% of all reps fail to hit their annual sales targets. The average New Years Resolution lasts until January 12th. There has to be a better way to make a choice pick a goal and hold ourselves accountable to hitting the target. Show up and learn how to set a system that will keep you on track and help you hit the targets you choose.

An example of a medium threshold offer to attend
a class or webinar in a group setting.

Matt • 1st
Sales Trainer and Coach to Indianapolis Businesses at Sandler Training DTB
22h

Sign up today for our Sandler Training Sales Bootcamp on Friday, December 7th 9 am to 4 pm at #SandlerTraining DTB #Indianapolis Boot Camp Includes: Sandler Training materials, DISC behavioral assessment and private (...see more

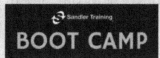

An example of a medium-high threshold offer to invest
in a one-day boot camp to sample the sales training.

Chapter Six

How to Sell More by Working Less Hard

L et's be honest, spending day after day calling strangers and getting rejected is not much different than other forms of hard labor.

Sure, it's not as physically strenuous as building houses, roads, or cars, but it can be less fulfilling.

Try walking up to a construction worker on a scorching hot day, who's been up since dawn – sweating, carrying lumber, hammering nails, and getting yelled at by their foreman.

Now go ask that construction worker to trade places with you for just one week.

Instead of that dusty worksite, he can go to your spotless, air-conditioned office and sip free coffee – but – must call 100 strangers, land some appointments, then sell something or risk making NO money and possibly losing their job.

My bet is he will stick with the construction job.

The truth is most salespeople don't like cold calling and aren't any good at it. I know I don't like it, and even after 20+ years in sales, I'm still not very good at it.

We all get into sales to have fun, make money, interact with people, make a difference – and work hard for sure. We thrive on competition and the challenge of closing a sale.

Getting stuck with cold calling as the only way to develop new business is the biggest reason talented people avoid the selling profession – or leave the profession.

As we covered in Part One, *selling* is persuading a qualified lead on the merits of your product or service. This takes skill, experience, passion, and a focused, persistent effort. **This alone can be an exhaustive process.**

Marketing is creating a selling scenario – an opportunity, a meeting, an open door – so you can begin the process of *persuasion*.

To do this effectively, and consistently, on top of the selling part, has become more work than any one person can handle *successfully and for very long* without burning out.

Curiously, I have been in B2B sales for most of my career and have yet to work for an employer who separates these two functions! Because marketing didn't use to be necessary, selling didn't used to require so much labor.

My first professional sales job after college was selling advertising for *The Indianapolis Star* newspaper. They were THE dominant force in local news and advertising.

Here's some helpful advice: If you can sell for a monopoly like newspapers were in those days, do it. *Everyone* read our paper back then.

I could stop in, unannounced, to almost *any* business, and speak to a <u>business owner</u>. Because I represented the newspaper, they'd often complain to me about our obnoxious sports columnist – the late great Robin Miller – who everyone despised, yet they religiously read his columns (meaning he was terrific at his job). I'd spend 10–20 minutes chatting about the news of the day, then naturally steer them toward the benefits of running ads in the paper – and often make a sale.

Selling newspaper advertising was easier because there were fewer advertising choices, and business owners were more accessible. This was before digital marketing, before cable and satellite expanded to hundreds of channels, and before streaming services, like Netflix were around. And just as importantly, and this gets overlooked by many selling organizations today: This was before the massive corporate consolidation of many smaller businesses into larger centralized conglomerates, shifting a lot of decision making out smaller markets.

I wasn't making cold calls; even when I called on complete strangers, **they knew I was from the only paper in town**. And you know what?

- Selling was a joy.
- I loved my job.
- I looked forward to Mondays.

- I crushed my sales goals.
- I truly enjoyed new business development!

In four glorious years working at *The Indianapolis Star,* I won **Salesperson of the Year** twice. I imagined being in the newspaper business for the rest of my life and wished it would've worked out, but unfortunately, today newspapers are a shadow of their former selves.

Today, newspaper reps spend much more time and energy (labor) just getting the attention of their prospective clients. This is the kind of labor I'm talking about, and pretty much in every industry today, business owners and decision makers have more choices and are busier than ever.

Today, when you choose to forage for clients using only cold outreach, you are choosing to do hard labor when more productive methods are available.

Chapter Seven

How Apple Makes It Easy for Prospects to Avoid You

Truth is, most of us don't like being sold to. But we do like to buy!

Do you look forward to buying a car? Some relish it, most don't. In fact, many dread the process of buying a car.

And because of this, finally, after decades of torture from greedy car dealers, the process of buying a car has changed.

There's a company called Carvana where you can buy a car online, have it delivered, and never talk to a salesperson face to face.

And technology, like the

Every smartphone offers you the option of blocking calls.

smartphone and the internet, allows you to avoid salespeople altogether.

When I was growing up (in the 1980s) EVERYBODY answered their phones AND returned their messages.

You really didn't have a choice because before smart phones, the phone would just ring and ring and ring.

Heck, we didn't even know who was calling – and that was part of the fun!

It was considered impolite – even if someone was trying to sell you something – to ignore a ringing telephone.

Today, thanks largely to Apple and their smartphones, everyone, even my grandma, can:

- See who's calling.
- Ignore calls (even from friends) and not seem impolite.
- Mute their phones.
- Block calls from strangers.
- Block calls from anyone, even friends.
- Ignore voicemails too.

Today, people who value their time don't allow random calls to interrupt their day.

If you are calling prospects *cold* on their cell phones, you will likely be <u>blocked or silenced</u>. And if you are emailing prospective clients out of the blue, your emails are likely getting caught up in a spam filter.

It's likely most your prospects are not even conscious of your *cold* efforts to reach them!

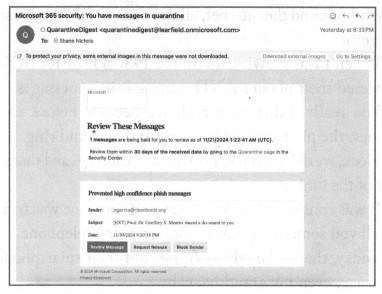

*My work email filters just about every email
coming from someone I don't know.*

Think about that for a minute. Let that sink in.

**It's likely most your prospects are not even
conscious of your *cold* efforts to reach them!**

Tell me, if you can't reach your prospect, how in the heck
are you ever going to sell them anything?

There is a monumental shift occurring in our economy
right now, spurred on not only by the pandemic but also
technology, and it is permanently altering how people prefer
to buy and sell.

We are moving away from a manual process of buying
stuff. Younger generations prefer a more <u>automated</u> and
technology-driven way of buying through websites, apps,
texts, emails, and video calls versus the *in-person experience*
favored by older generations.

It's not because the old ways don't work. It's because the new ways are more efficient, easier, cheaper, and safer.

I sell corporate sponsorship for a Division I NCAA athletics program. My clients are business owners who want to tap into the power of our fanbase.

Ten years ago, most of our clients went to the games and lived in town; negotiations were done in person, often over lunch. Today, very few of my clients attend our games. They are busy with their kids or prefer to watch the game on TV, from the comfort of their home. Many don't live here, and most of our communication is done via the phone or email.

In my first year on the job, my two largest clients (both banks) were acquired by larger banks from other cities. Corporate consolidation is the #1 reason we lose sponsors. It removes decision making from a smaller market like mine, to a centralized corporate office somewhere else, making it harder to access decisions makers, and requiring a different approach.

Our clients still recognize the value of sports marketing; *they just buy it differently than they did 10 years ago.* And the tools that guide decision-making are changing too – and *have* changed for many already.

Older generations, like the Baby Boomers and Gen X, for example, still may take your cold call, if you can get past their receptionist. These veterans of business still like to kick the tires and joust with salespeople.

Younger generations ... Millennials and Gen Z ... prefer having more control over the buying process. They seek out

---

helpful information *first* before talking to a salesperson, which is easy to find on the internet.

The guiding influence is Amazon who offers **an abundance of lower threshold information** for all products and services. Before you buy on Amazon you can view a product from different angles and colors, read samples of books, watch videos, and read customer reviews.

The point here is that you can use technology to your advantage or your disadvantage. And all the benefits of technology work against you when cold calling.

Chapter Eight

The Biggest, Most Obvious, Yet Overlooked Secrets to Being a Successful Salesperson

Over the last four chapters, I have outlined the major reasons why you shouldn't spend any of your precious time cold calling prospects:

- It only serves to eliminate the 99% of potential prospects who aren't ready yet to meet or talk to a salesperson.
- It can be labor-intensive drudgery that should be replaced with marketing.
- Technology enables younger generations to pretty much avoid or ignore most cold outreach efforts.
- Chasing people devalues your position, making it harder to establish trust and credibility.

The single biggest reward for never cold calling again is this: **FOCUS.**

Recognizing and then abandoning unproductive behavior will create more time to focus on the most important people in your work life – your current customers.

I can't count how many times I've bought a car, an insurance policy, a roof, a computer, a printer, and all sorts of other expensive things, and never heard back from the people who sold me those items. That's common in the consumer world but doesn't make it right.

In the B2B world, it's also common for salespeople to move on to their next cold pursuit rather than focus inward and embrace the potential of nurturing their existing clients.

A focus on *over-delivering* for your current clients will lead to easy renewals, upsells, and referrals – the most profitable and lowest-labor growth you can generate.

And you will have more time to focus on converting your warm leads (people in your pipeline who will meet with you) into new clients.

If you think about it, the secret to being successful in sales boils down to these two things:

1. **Spend more time coming up with ways of converting leads into clients – those people in your pipeline willing to meet with you.**
2. **Spend more time amazing, nurturing, and upselling existing clients.**

These two groups, I'll bet you, comprise more than 80% of your profits and sales.

And if you plow 80% of your time back into just these two groups, your return on investment will far exceed any luck you stumble upon while cold calling.

For example, next time someone gives you an opportunity to present and sell them something, blow their socks off!

Do some advance research and talk to their customers. Read their trade publications and understand the economic trends in their industry.

Know *their* competitors and know what *your* competitors are offering them. Anticipate objections and address them in your presentation.

Brainstorm ideas that can measurably improve their business, and mock-up these ideas into visuals that bring them to life. Don't settle for slide after slide of text in a PowerPoint® presentation. Rather, commit to delivering something visually stunning with mock-ups and illustrations.

Ironically, the biggest obstacle to spending more time and effort on existing customers and your warmest prospects *is the constant distraction and pressure of having to develop new business!*

Regrettably, it's easy to adopt the behavior of a dog, always chasing that car down the road, straying farther and farther away from the riches in their own backyard.

Refraining from cold outreach opens the door to spending more time on proven, profitable behaviors such as:

- Deepening relationships with existing customers.
- Nurturing, delighting, and surprising existing customers.

- Collecting referrals from existing clients.
- Upselling existing clients.
- Collecting testimonials and proof your product or service works.
- Unearthing pain experienced by warm prospects.
- Brainstorming ideas to reduce or eliminate this pain.
- Learning more about marketing and how to create compelling sales angles and hooks (more on this in Part Three).
- Creating ways to position yourself as a value provider and authority, rather than just another salesperson.

For the past decade I have committed significant time and effort learning and practicing these methods. I stopped cold calling. I resisted the urge to spend time on prospects who weren't actual leads and dedicated myself to marketing and lead generation.

And now in Part Three, I'll share how I used my lead generation marketing to replace cold calling and cold emailing.

PART THREE

How to Get Appointments with Time-Starved, Hard-to-Reach Business Owners and Decision Makers

In Part One, I pointed out the most challenging obstacle facing sales professionals, today is not the actual selling part; the tough part is *getting in front of* a qualified prospect.

And in Part Two, hopefully, I convinced you that cold calling and emailing complete strangers is no longer an effective use of your time.

This section is where I share what I've learned about getting the attention of time-starved, hard to reach business owners and decision makers.

I've read every significant book ever published on sales, direct-response marketing, copywriting, and invested thousands of my own hard-earned dollars into countless courses and seminars.

I'll share my story of going from *chasing* to **attracting** clients, and reveal how through marketing, I'm able to generate leads from the right kind of prospects, spending less time cold prospecting, and more time <u>selling</u>.

Chapter Nine

How I Took Control and Stopped Cold Calling

In 2018 I went back to selling TV advertising after working in client services for an advertising agency.

I missed the challenge and freedom of sales. I relished the test of building up a book of business and working on straight commission.

Call me crazy, but I chose a new business development position over one that paid a salary and offered an established account list. Looking back, it was a mistake.

I chose this 100% commission path because it offered unlimited earning potential, plus more freedom and flexibility. Besides, I was full of confidence from my previous success in selling TV advertising.

But I vastly underestimated how difficult it would be.

There is nothing harder in sales than starting from scratch, especially if you work for an employer that doesn't understand or invest in lead generation marketing.

I remember those first few months: I would book a conference room at the TV station and force myself to cold call for about an hour each day.

On top of that, I would send 10 to 20 cold emails each morning, then drop in on car dealers and other retailers (unannounced canvassing), hoping to land a few minutes with a buyer.

Even working for the #1 TV station in the city – an NBC affiliate with over a million viewers per week – it was still a struggle to land appointments with good prospects.

The selling landscape had clearly changed while I was away from sales. My selling skills weren't the problem. Sure, I was a bit rusty, but I could still sell. *My problem was getting my foot in the door with qualified prospects.*

Just a decade ago, selling TV advertising was easier. There were fewer choices, fewer TV stations for sure, and no streaming services like Netflix.

Today, digital advertising choices continue to multiply, from Facebook to Google and so many more, all taking a bigger slice of local marketing budgets.

I noticed business owners are simply busier than they were 10 years ago. They are inundated by salespeople from every conceivable angle. This is what I estimate an average business owner is experiencing daily:

- **Credit card processing:** 5 to 10 different salespeople calling and or emailing.
- **Promotional or sign companies:** 1 to 2 different salespeople calling and or emailing.

- **Advertising:** 5 to 10 different salespeople calling and or emailing.
- **Office supplies:** 1 to 2 different salespeople calling and or emailing.
- **Banking:** 1 to 2 different salespeople calling and or emailing.
- **Software:** 5 to 10 different salespeople calling and or emailing.
- **Printers:** 1 to 2 different salespeople calling and or emailing.
- **Accounting services**: 1 to 2 different salespeople calling and or emailing.
- **Charitable or community related**: 2 to 3 different organizations calling/emailing.
- **Industry specific products/services**: 2 to 3 different salespeople calling and or emailing.

It's not uncommon for business owners to hear from 30 or more different salespeople <u>on any given day</u>. Crazy, right?

Building up my book of business from scratch with cold calling and cold emailing seemed like an uphill battle.

Miserable, and searching for new ideas, this is the moment I stumbled upon Dan Kennedy and two of his amazing books:

- *No B.S. Direct Marketing: For Non-Direct Marketing Businesses, Third Edition*
- *No B.S. Sales Success in the New Economy*

What I learned is the smartest sales organizations don't just *chase* prospects with cold outreach; they figure out ways to **attract** them.

Attract rather than *chase*.

And those who do this effectively are all good at *marketing* – but not just any kind of marketing.

They are good at *direct-response marketing*. Most of the marketing you see every day is brand marketing, or *branding*.

And in brand advertising, usually there is no offer, no persuasive copy, no reason to respond (today), and no effort to capture contact information.

Generally, in branding there is no way to measure response. Coca-Cola advertising is a perfect example of brand advertising. They spend billions each year just to make you feel good about their brand, and rarely is there any trackable offer, or even a coupon.

Direct-response advertising, on the other hand, is all about generating a measurable result, and in B2B marketing, the result we want is a *qualified lead* or an *inquiry*.

Fisher Investments is a great example of a direct-response marketer with only one goal: Capture a qualified prospect's contact information.

And to do this, they entice you with free information in the form of a helpful guide: ***"99 Tips to Make Your Retirement More Comfortable."***

If you're near retirement age, reading this magazine, and stumble upon this ad, you might be interested in those 99 tips. And notice they don't require you to speak to a salesperson to read the report. A perfect example of a low-threshold strategy designed to generate more interest from buyers in every stage of the buying process.

Also, in their advertising they will qualify **who** they want to respond: *investors with $500k or more in investable assets.* If you don't have that much to invest, don't bother requesting their guide, keeping unqualified prospects away.

I was very skeptical about my ability to make direct-response marketing work. People have been selling TV advertising the same way for decades. You pound the pavement, make your calls, end of story.

*A Fishers Investments direct response ad I
ripped out of a Forbes magazine.*

So, I decided to try one of the oldest B2B direct-response marketing tactics: **The Sales Letter.**

Yes, a real letter on a piece of paper sent in an envelope with a stamp. I reasoned: if I send prospects a letter before I call them, it will set me apart and warm up my cold call.

And if my letter said something compelling, something

helpful, something addressing their pain and needs, I might even get them to respond.

Also, NONE of my competitors were sending letters.

If you think about it, the mailbox has become the least crowded place to reach business owners and decision makers.

Buyers are overwhelmed with technology (email, instant messenger, social media). But their mailboxes are mostly empty, maybe a few bills and magazines.

And don't confuse my sales letter with junk mail; it's the opposite of junk mail (more on how to craft a sales letter guaranteed to be opened and read by your prospects in Chapter 16).

I remembered another quote from Dan Kennedy that he would emphasize over and over in several of his books and speeches:

"Show up where (and when) no one else is…"

And everyone else was showing up in *email*.

So, I decided I would now show up in the **mailbox**.

This led me to another book (by guess who … Dan Kennedy!) that helped me become a better writer, which may be the most overlooked skill salespeople need today: *The Ultimate Sales Letter*.

It taught me how to write a letter (and emails) that get the attention of stressed-out, time-starved business owners, and if the letter is good enough, it'll even get them to *respond* to it. Imagine that!

How is this possible? By writing persuasively, creatively,

and understanding the pain my prospects deal with every day, and most importantly, distilling their pain into an angle (or hook) that gets their attention.

My First Sales Letter...

I've spent most of my sales career not really saying anything different from my competitors. In fact, prospects pretty much tune us out because they've literally *heard it all* by now.

So, after thinking long and hard and interviewing several clients, I figured out the issues our prospective TV advertising clients were dealing with as it pertained to local advertising.

Overall, they:

1. Are overwhelmed by the number of places they could advertise.
2. Didn't know how (or where) to reach their target customers anymore.
3. Felt pressure to spend on digital and social media because their competitors were all doing it and so were their peers.
4. Didn't have the time or know-how to measure their advertising.
5. Feared of missing out on the next new digital or social media thing, like TikTok® for example.

The sales angle I decided to use in my letter to hook clients was Warren Buffett.

Warren Buffett, The Oracle of Omaha

I compared buying advertising to buying stocks and urged clients to become *value investors* just like him, the most famous investor in the world. Value investors (like Buffett) search for stocks snubbed by the public, stocks that can be bought below their basic value, therefore increasing the chances to earn a profit.

These value stocks are often boring but profitable businesses – and well managed – just overlooked by the media and mainstream investors who want something *sexier*.

Uber is an example of a stock the public is fascinated with (but not Buffett). If the public backs a stock, the price has usually been driven up too high for a value investor to make serious money.

But a railroad company, for example – something boring, industrial yet profitable and reliable – is an "Oracle of Omaha" – type investment. In fact, Buffett does own railroads!

My two-page letter pointed out that the advertising world – just like the stock market – has never been more confusing. And if Buffett were buying advertising today, he'd forget all the hype around the latest digital and social media fads and **focus on value**. I even included his picture in the letter to drive home the point.

I reasoned, while TV advertising is far from perfect, there is still tremendous value left for opportunistic advertisers. And because all the other advertisers were in a frenzy over digital advertising, TV has never been more affordable.

The letter followed a structure, one that anyone can copy, and it:

1. Grabbed their attention with a catchy headline.
2. Identified the real pain going on in advertisers' minds.
3. Provided a solution to cure the pain – in this case the "hook" or selling angle was to think of local advertising as the stock market, and to become a value investor instead of chasing digital and social fads.
4. Backed it up with third-party evidence, like research and testimonials from other advertisers.
5. Utilized direct-response design enhancements, like pictures and headlines.
6. Provided a low-threshold way of interacting with me – research the TV station already subscribed to.
7. Also provided a higher-threshold way of interacting with me – my email address.

I mailed my letter to about 50 prospects, and it exceeded my expectations. One owner of a large residential plumbing operation (a guy bombarded by salespeople every day, someone who's ignored countless emails and cold calls from me) **responded AND complimented me on the letter,** *saying I was right on the money* and wanted to meet*!*

I knew I was onto something. This guy chose me over dozens of other salespeople, took time out of his busy day, raised his hand, and said, *"Yeah, I'm interested. Please follow up!"*

It was all because he got an old-fashioned, personal letter from me in the mail. Something I doubt any other salesperson took the time to do.

On almost the same day the owner of the plumbing company responded to my letter, I was offered a new career opportunity. I left the TV station to go sell corporate sponsorships for Ball State Athletics, my alma mater.

This new job gave me the perfect opportunity to continue with my lead generation marketing, and in the next chapter, I'll show you how it worked.

P.S. Writing sales letters is not required, it's one of many available *marketing tactics* you can use to position yourself as a value provider, and land more appointments with higher quality prospects! Please read on!

Chapter Ten

Whoever Can Spend the Most Money Attracting (and keeping) Clients ... Wins

This concept may seem foreign, or even crazy to you. And there is a good chance your boss will think it's ludicrous! That's ok, read on.

I've noticed, when someone from a traditional sales background is first introduced to this idea, they often dismiss it.

It's natural to resist change. But there is a difference between resisting change, and just being stuck. You need to move beyond your limiting beliefs, and past the limiting beliefs of others, even when they're your friends, co-workers – even your boss.

You can be friends with them, but don't let their limited views limit your income. They must not have the desire to learn; they probably don't read books, or invest in education, or anything else for that matter. They probably spend a lot of their free time watching TV and scrolling through social media.

The good news is, because this requires some investment on your part, very few of your competitors (and fellow salespeople) will do anything like this. *That's what, in part, makes this your competitive advantage.*

Spend Money to Get the Attention of your Best Prospects

I admit, it took me some time to fully embrace this concept as well, and that is: *to get the attention of your most prized prospects, you should willingly spend money getting their attention, which becomes your competitive advantage in the marketplace.*

Why is it a competitive advantage? Because spending money buys speed, it reduces the time and labor required to get appointments with good prospects. It buys you time to spend on more profitable activities like closing sales with warm prospects, and upselling existing clients.

What do I mean by spending money? Well, rather than engaging in random acts of prospecting … like cold calling and cold emailing … I'm urging you to invest in **marketing campaigns** designed to attract the attention of your best prospects.

A good campaign should include direct, targeted, and persuasive messaging sent over a specific time period. The best tactics for creating an effective campaign are covered extensively in the rest of this book.

If done correctly, your marketing efforts will result in

a small percentage of prospects *seeking you out and asking you for an appointment*! Imagine that. **Yes,** it is possible, I'm doing it regularly today, and I will show you proof.

If your marketing produces no immediate response, that is perfectly fine because the true intent and advantage is this effort <u>warms up</u> your prospects like nothing else, so when you do follow up, you are no longer making a cold attempt. Your investment has *earned you the right to call on this prospect*!

This marketing also magically elevates your positioning, giving you more confidence while showing your prospects you mean business, and refuse to be ignored!

You may still get a NO, but … you will vastly increase the odds of getting a response, and more appointments. Besides, a no this year can turn into a *YES* next year. This effort builds long-term equity in the minds of your prospects.

How Can YOU Possibly Afford to Spend Money Attracting Clients?

First let's cover how you **can** afford to do this, profitably, and it helps if you have some of these key ingredients:

1. A high average sale – four to five figures ideally.
2. A healthy gross profit margin on your product or service.
3. A high average customer lifetime value.
4. Ascension, a way of enticing customers to spend more money in the future.

It all boils down to the fact that the most expensive

and time-consuming thing to do in sales is to acquire new customers, but once you have a customer, the world can be your oyster.

They can buy from you FOREVER, and that's where the *real money* is. The back end, or the lifetime value of each customer. That's why finding ways for every customer to spend more with you is so important – it recoups your front-end marketing costs.

The Math Behind Spending to Get the Appointment

When I began selling sponsorships for Ball State Athletics, my average sale was about $12,000. The amount of profit for each sponsorship deal varies. Our custom packages can include radio, signage, social media, display ads, print ads, on-site promotions, and more.

In addition to having an average sale in the five figures, and a decent gross profit margin, most of our clients sign multi-year deals. Everyone has different numbers and different scenarios; I'm providing a very general peek into the math of my specific business. It's vitally important you understand these metrics in your own business:

1. My average sale = $12,000
2. My lifetime average value of each new client = $36,000 (over 3 years). Often, we can get them to renew another term, so the actual lifetime value of can easily climb into six figures.
3. Whenever a sponsorship is up for renewal, we are always presenting ideas to increase their spending.

So, let's review:

Knowing this math, and the potential of each sale, *it makes my sponsorship packages a perfect situation to invest money attracting clients.* AND I can keep investing provided my marketing continues to produce results!

Now, imagine this scenario. A national marketer with no geographic boundaries with an average customer value (like mine) *could* profitably spend as much as $12,000 to attract *each client*.

How could they do that?

Because of the math. They know (long term) if they spend $12,000 to get a new customer, and if each customer spends hundreds of thousands of dollars in their lifetime, *and* they can reliably acquire more customers just like this, *then* they can adjust their operation to absorb short-term losses and reap the long-term revenue. And why would they do that? Because it's a **competitive advantage** to outspend your competitors attracting new customers! They're buying speed and time!

In my situation, I can't spend thousands of dollars on every new customer for a variety of reasons: in part, because there is only so much demand I can create for sponsorship in Ball State Athletics – our geographic footprint is limited.

BUT ... *I can spend enough money to make my job easier AND to rise above my local direct and indirect competitors,* especially those selling other marketing opportunities and sponsorships. In my situation, I only need to spend between $20 to $50 per prospect.

This Concept Is Not New or Untested

Gaining a competitive advantage by spending money on marketing is not an untested strategy. But I find it hard for those stuck in the blue-collar selling world to accept this idea.

Many sales organizations are addicted to the *perceived* savings of cold outreach. But cold calling is far from free, it saps time and energy away from more productive efforts – like closing, and the retention and upselling of existing clients. Of course, there is a risk that your marketing efforts won't work. But I can guarantee this, it gives you the right to follow up, it warms up prospects unlike anything else.

That's why I wrote this book, because if someone like me, with my traditional sales background, can make this work in a recovering rust-belt town in Muncie, IN. then you can make it work anywhere, in any type of business.

If you look to the consumer world (B2C), there are many examples of spending money as a competitive advantage. Do you notice many soda companies breaking through Coke's (and Pepsi's) dominance?

Do you see Coca-Cola or Pepsi hoarding their money and not spending anything on advertising? Nope, **they spend as much money as they can possibly afford** to remain top-of-mind to any soda drinker, *making it as difficult as possible for any other competitor to gain market share.*

Amazon spends gobs of money *and* is unprofitable in many of their businesses – including their streaming service. But their front-end investment in original content and the NFL pays dividends in the long run, on the back end it generates new members for their Prime membership program. It also *retains* members, who pay an annual fee, and spend more on everything because of their membership.

Have you ever heard of Grant Cardone? If you pay any attention to social media, you've heard of Grant. He's a sales trainer and real estate investor, and he spends millions each year attracting clients.

I've seen videos of him onstage at his popular 10X sales seminar. When somebody in the audience complains they can't break through with a prospect on the phone, Grant will cold call that prospect on the spot and land an appointment – or a sale. It's a cool demonstration, and Grant is good, **but he's also a celebrity**, a status and position he's built through his marketing efforts.

What's funny is, <u>I doubt Grant has made a cold call himself in decades</u>. He's too smart to waste his time on that high-labor drudgery. His true secret to success? He sells high-ticket, high-profit things, and he markets them extremely well, producing tons leads for his sales teams to follow up on. I'll also bet you his sales team makes zero cold calls, but they do spend a lot of time FOLLOWING UP ON LEADS. A much more efficient process.

I've mentioned Salesforce already; the software company is a leader in using marketing to attract prospects. And one of their favorite tactics is having big swanky events, featuring some of their best clients and prospects *as speakers*, while inviting the rest of their best prospects to attend.

While all your competitors are spinning their wheels with cold outreach and weak pitches, create your own marketing campaign to stand out from the crowd, and

GET THE APPOINTMENT, make more money, and hit your sales goals, all with much less manual labor.

A Few Profitable Ways of Spending Money to Get the Appointment

1. Create marketing and outreach campaigns with strong sales copy using a variety of media if possible. In the coming chapters you'll see my favorite tactics and sales angles that can be applied to any selling situation.

2. Whatever you decide to send a prospect, *do it in a way that bypasses gatekeepers*, and is guaranteed to be read by your prospect, by using one or more of these:

    a. USPS First-Class Mail works well; don't use their Bulk Mail. Even better, use...

    b. USPS Priority Mail. This is a big cardboard envelope with tracking, but even better, try...

    c. FedEx – 100% guaranteed to get opened by whoever you are targeting.

3. Sponsor something your decision maker cares about; attend their functions. A charity, arts organization, Little League baseball—whatever. Appear on their radar!

4. Hire a speaker (somebody your prospects are interested in), have an event, and invite prospects. Heck, want to be bold? Hire your prospect to speak!

Read their trade journals, and benefit from being the provider of value.

These are just some of your options. The point is, the business that can spend the most on acquiring a new customer has the competitive advantage in the marketplace, so become this type of business.

In the next chapter, I'll introduce you to the most successful way of attracting prospects into your world, and possibly the single best investment you can make in your effort to get the attention of your best prospects.

Chapter Eleven

How to Use Lead Magnets to Attract Prospective Clients

The most important thing I've learned about B2B marketing is, if you want to attract clients – rather than chase them – you need good bait.

It's no different than fishing. You need bait to catch fish, and different kinds of bait attract different kinds of fish.

If you want to catch bluegill, use live worms. If you want to catch muskie, cast a large, fake, bedazzled lure – and have patience.

And if you want to attract quality B2B leads, you'll need something called a **lead magnet**.

Successful examples include:

1. Research reports
2. White papers
3. Books
4. Interactive games

5. Quizzes
6. Webinars
7. Seminars
8. Live demonstrations
9. Audio content
10. Video content
11. Events

The most effective lead magnets offer helpful information where prospective buyers can learn about your product or service, or trends in their industry, in a *low-threshold manner* before an interaction with a salesperson is required.

This lower threshold bridge will attract more potential buyers who are in various stages of their buying journey. Back in Chapter 5, when I described how Sandler sales trainer Matt Nettleton develops new business, he uses books, guides, webinars and boot camps as lead magnets.

So, rather than calling prospects cold, you can begin to **advertise your lead magnet**. You'll get more response by *promoting* a helpful, low threshold educational bridge than you will just asking for appointments or consultations.

Your educational tool (or activity) offers value without the stress of dealing with a salesperson, it alleviates the fear of *being sold*. You are choosing to be part of the entire buying journey, not just the end.

Another benefit of a lead magnet? It positions you in a different light – instead of a chasing salesperson (a dog) you become an attractive value provider (a cat).

The key exchange here is a prospect will share their

contact information to access your lead magnet. This is called *opting-in* and becomes your permission to follow up.

The most advanced marketers create automated follow-up sequences, usually a combination of email and snail mail, where clients (who opted-in) are fed a continuous stream of helpful information meant to move them toward an appointment or outright sale.

Your lead magnet's ability to attract prospects is based on how valuable the content or experience is to the prospect.

I live in Indianapolis, where a software start-up called Pattern 89 helped publishers and marketers choose the highest performing images for digital publishing and advertising.

Their software used artificial intelligence (robots) to analyze millions of data points in a variety of online settings. For example, the right picture can boost readership for an article or sales of a product.

Software is a complicated and hyper-competitive industry, and most software companies – especially startups – all use some form of lead generation marketing to help with new business development efforts. Startups can't afford to waste time having their salespeople make cold calls. They hire salespeople to close!

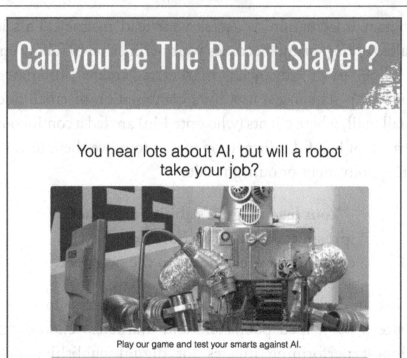

Pattern 89's primary lead magnet, a
quiz – The Robot Slayer.

Pattern 89 used a variety of lead magnets; my favorite was their quiz –**The Robot Slayer.** It tested your ability to choose the highest performing images against their better-informed robots.

I took the quiz several times, it was a fun way of learning more about the power of artificial intelligence. And I couldn't beat their robots, who toppled my human instincts with their ability to analyze tons of data in seconds.

Using this lead magnet, Pattern 89 demonstrated the power of their software in a low-threshold way – without requiring me to talk to a salesperson as the first and only step. This helped attract a larger number of prospects into their sales funnel or pipeline.

After I took the quiz, I was added to their email list, then began receiving additional helpful emails and invitations to webinars. And *then* a salesperson emailed me, but I didn't respond. Since I didn't respond or engage with any of their follow-up efforts, I was removed from their prospect list because I didn't prove I was worth any further effort.

All of this was done *without any labor or cold outreach*, using technology and marketing to position themselves to prospective clients *and* to efficiently qualify them. While the writing of this book, their sales strategy must have worked, because they were acquired by a larger corporation (Shutterstock®) for millions of dollars.

Are you still not convinced lead magnets work? Ever heard of McKinsey & Company?

How the Most Successful B2B (In the World) Finds New Clients

How does the world's most successful consulting firm find new business?

Arguably, McKinsey & Company is the most influential most profitable B2B in existence. I can tell you for certain, they do not cold call or cold email anybody. So, how do they attract clients?

You might be thinking … McKinsey is uber-successful; they don't need to find new business. It finds them. This is true, demonstrated and publicized *success* is a form of client attraction.

But they had to start from somewhere. And their strategy from the beginning was to publish and attract clients with **thought-leadership**.

From the beginning they used educational bridges (lead magnets) helping buyers on their journey in a variety of targeted industries. Today they publish 40+ different email newsletters and alerts. They have their own Insights Store – essentially a bookstore.

They continually produce valuable insights and position themselves as a trusted authority in the business world. And before potential clients can access their educational bridges, they must submit their contact information, supplying a steady flow of leads to follow up with.

This is how one of the most successful companies in the world generates leads. While simultaneously positioning themselves to command premium fees in a very competitive marketplace. This same strategy is repeated in some way, shape, or form all the most successful selling organizations.

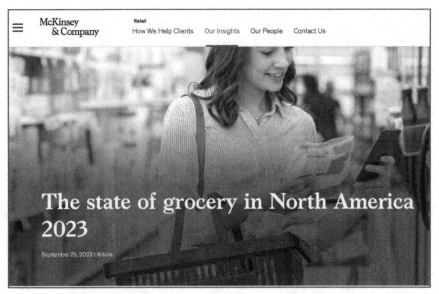

One example of a report published by Mckinsey &
Company which helps them attract clients. They don't
cold call, but you must submit your email address
before you can download, so they will follow up!

Don't let the idea of publishing something interesting and helpful intimidate you. You can easily outsource this effort to professional writers and marketers. I am not a professional writer, but in the next chapter, I will share how I created my first lead magnet, which allowed me to start attracting clients. And if I can do this, so can you.

Chapter Twelve

How I Built My First Lead Magnet

Inspired to build my own lead magnet, I started researching the pain our sponsorship clients were dealing with as it related to local marketing.

If you remember the first sales letter I wrote while selling TV advertising, my hook (or sales angle) was for advertisers to imagine themselves as value investors like Warren Buffett. And to consider TV advertising as an undervalued, contrarian investment. In my Buffett themed-letter, I played up this hook by stoking the emotions of safety, reliability, credibility, being a contrarian, and investing at a low price with high return.

This hook (or sales angle) is just a way of getting attention. I believe all new business development requires some g hook or sales angle these days. It will vastly increase the likelihood of you getting a response, and an appointment.

Now here's where another book helped me, by expert

copywriter John Carlton: *Kick-Ass Copywriting Secrets of a Marketing Rebel*.

Carlton says imagine it's a Thursday evening after work, and you meet up with your favorite client at the local watering hole. After a few drinks, your client starts to loosen up a bit and candidly spills all his doubts and fears as it relates to your product or service. The goal here is to tap into their true pain, or **hot buttons**, because <u>what fuels decision-making is rarely what we sellers assume</u>, since so few of us have walked in the shoes of our clients.

Information (or bait) that elicits a response from busy people requires real insight into their worlds.

And if throwing back a few cocktails helps you uncover this information more effectively, all the better.

This took me some time, several interviews (drinks) with my clients, and I'm continually refining it. But eventually, I landed on a few hot buttons as they pertain to buying a sponsorship with Ball State Athletics:

1. Ball State University is in Muncie, IN, a recovering Rust Belt industrial town whose economy is now largely dependent on the university and a few other employers.
2. Because of the decline of traditional media, the local newspaper, the campus newspaper, and local radio no longer effectively or efficiently reach the most affluent people in Muncie. And the most affluent folks are associated with the university in some

way (employees, visitors, students, etc.). I need to position sponsorship as the premiere platform to connect with the Ball State Community – my own term for the most affluent group in the region.

3. Many business owners believe it's tough to track or get measurable results with sponsorships, especially sports sponsorships. Therefore, I must prove we can.

4. Many of our clients are alumni and consider sponsorship as a community service or as support for their school, rather than a marketing investment competing with other advertising expenditures. To unlock more money, I need to reposition sponsorship as a marketing investment.

5. Most prospects don't grasp or appreciate the economic impact Ball State University has on their business. Some even have strong emotions against the university for a variety of reasons. So, I must remind them their future growth depends on courting our community.

Next, Carlton suggests distilling these hot buttons into an elevator-style pitch, like this:

Structure of an Elevator Pitch

A. I help (group of people)
B. Do/Get (benefit)
C. Better/Cheaper/Faster/Easier
D. Even if (worst-case scenario)

So, I plugged my nuggets of truth into my own elevator pitch, and it has become my underlying hook or angle for all my marketing:

The Ball State Athletics Sponsorship Pitch:

A. I can help your business...
B. Profit from the Ball State Community, the largest, most affluent economic force in the region – a market you should be actively courting if you want to grow and prosper here ...
C. Better, cheaper, and more efficiently than any other media or advertising.
D. Even if you've tried sponsorship with us in the past and it has failed.
E. I guarantee we can make it work for your business, measurably.

And then I created a lead magnet addressing these hot buttons. I created a guide and called it: ***The 10 Ways to Profit from Ball State with Sports Sponsorship.*** My 41-page guide highlights the 10 unique benefits of tapping into the largest economic force in their community – Ball State University – and the only Division I NCAA program. It includes lots of photos, a sales letter, research, testimonials from existing sponsors, endorsements from our athletics leadership, and an exclusive offer for new clients. At the end of this chapter, you can read Chapter 1 from the first edition of my guide – I am now in my 7th edition! You can access my latest edition by visiting www.ballstatesports. com/profit

I'll admit, this was a time-consuming activity – it took me a few months, and it continues to be a work in progress. While it's far from perfect, **it's good enough**, and I tweak it each year.

I get that not everyone likes to write, but writing a report or guide is just one kind of lead magnet. And if you look through mine, it's no literary work of art. This is a glorified PowerPoint presentation with more photos than words. Lead magnets don't need to be Pulitzer Prize-winning works of art to be successful. If you can pinpoint the real issues business owners are dealing with and offer sound solutions or advice, it really doesn't matter how you package it.

Lead magnets with impactful, relevant content can be as simple as short presentation or white paper detailing the top 5 trends in any industry.

But the real beauty of spending time and resources on creating a good lead magnet is it becomes an *evergreen asset* you can use repeatedly and then re-purpose into other forms of lead producing content. I created 10 different email blasts tied to each unique benefit, and 10 different sales letters.

If you can't ever see yourself writing a guide or report like this (or even hiring somebody to do it for you) a guide is just one type of lead magnet. My favorite lead magnet is a quiz, and in the next chapter you can see how I created my own.

This is the cover and image I used to promote my first lead magnet, my How to Profit Guide.

TOP 10 WAYS TO PROFIT

IDEA ONE

Profit by Utilizing Valuable Intellectual Property

One of the biggest challenges facing business owners today is figuring out how to differentiate themselves from their competitors. How can your law firm, furniture store, HVAC company, or auto dealership stand out from your competition?

Most local businesses say the same things in their advertising:

1. How long they've been in business
2. That they are a family-owned business
3. That they are locally owned and operated

Rarely are these features unique, and rarely compelling enough (on their own) to attract customers. If you think about it, successful national businesses aren't able to claim any of these features, and it doesn't seem to hurt them one bit.

Gone are the days when there was just one business in every category, leaving local customers few choices and options. A florist, dentist, grocery store, lawyer, accountant, furniture store hardware store .... all used to benefit from a lack of competition.

Every business and every category now have more local, national, and global competition than ever before. The one thing you can do as a business owner to stand out from this competition is attach yourself to something local, something near and dear to the hearts of thousands of potential customers.

And gaining the right to use the intellectual property of a brand that is near and dear to the hearts of hundreds of thousands of people is a proven step in this direction.

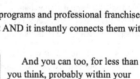

Sponsoring a major college sports program is a shortcut to the hard work it takes to develop your own unique selling point.

You gain access to a team's most valuable asset — their brand and logos. This means you can proclaim your business an official partner and incorporate these branded assets into your own advertising.

It creates *instant credibility* and a connection to their fan base, the community, alumni, university leadership, faculty, and students.

Nobody understands this better than the beverage industry. Pepsi may not taste like Coke, and Miller may not taste like Coors, but they are similar.

That's why these savvy marketers engage with college programs and professional franchises in just about every city — because it makes them stand out AND it instantly connects them with a large pool of customers.

And you can too, for less than you think, probably within your existing budget.

An even better idea is taking advantage of intellectual property and extending that to something you actually sell, like a physical product.

There are lots of applications – did you know that Toyota sells a Colts branded vehicle from their partnership with the Colts? The trucks feature Colt's trim and colors, and other special unique features and it commands a higher price than their other vehicles.

The same thing could be done on a smaller scale in East Central Indiana. A local car dealer could (and should) sell a Ball State branded car. I'll bet a new car decked out in Cardinal's red sporting a Charlie Cardinal badge would be a highly desirable item to thousands of local car buyers.

But this extends to all kinds of products and services, for example, a furniture store could create Ball State branded merchandise like recliners or furniture meant for dorm rooms. Banks and Credit Unions create branded credit and debit cards in an effort to appeal to the Ball State Community.

The simplest and easiest example of using intellectual property for your benefit is by displaying one of our Official Partners stickers on your place of business.

Bottom line, using intellectual property not only distinguishes you from competitors, but it also instantly creates credibility, and can even lead to direct profits from the sale of products.

Chapter Thirteen

How I Built My Second Lead Magnet

In addition to my *10 Ways to Profit* guide, I also created my own **Ball State Biz Quiz** as an additional lead magnet. I wanted more than one way for people to learn about sports sponsorship. Not everyone likes to read, and a quiz is more fun and interactive. You can also position it as an "assessment" rather than a quiz, suggesting there is a prescriptive value.

The beauty of a quiz is your questions can lead prospects to discovering they are a good fit for your product while also positioning you in a favorable light. For example, my questions (which you can view on the next few pages) point out specific benefits of sponsoring Ball State Athletics. And in many cases, it highlights the negatives of not being a sponsor, hopefully stoking some fear of missing out for their family, friends, and clients.

After a prospect completes my quiz, I'm notified via

email with their contact information, and they are presented with a variety of options to engage further.

The good news is quizzes are easy to create! And there are many software companies devoted to creating quizzes or assessments as lead magnets. I use **Lead Quizzes**, and it costs $49 per month.

Find my quiz here: www.ballstatesports.com/quiz

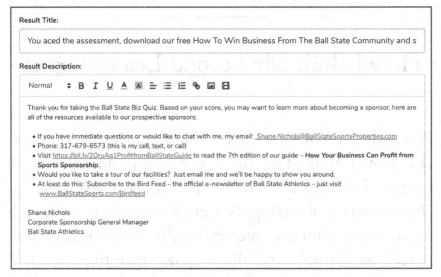

Once a prospect completes the quiz, they are provided an array of options to take the next step.

Here is the entire quiz along with the answers, and their respective point values. The higher the score, the more qualified the prospect.

----

1. Form Field – before taking the quiz I require a name and email address.

- First name:
- Work email address:

2. Are you a Ball State University Alumni? Either undergraduate or graduate degree or both?

- Yes = 10 points
- No = zero points

3. Describe your role in your business

    a. Owner/President = 10 points
    b. VP/Senior Decision Maker = 8 points
    c. Marketing Agency = 5 points
    d. Manager/Coordinator of Marketing = 3 points

4. Do you sell products and services to consumers (B2C), or do you sell to other businesses (B2B)?

    A. B2B = 5 points
    B. B2C = 5 points
    C. We cater to both B2B and B2C = 5 points

5. Do you buy any traditional local advertising? This could be local radio commercials, billboards, newspaper ads, direct mail or shared mail like Val Pak or Great Deals Magazine. This should include anything you spend marketing dollars on locally, including digital advertising like display ads, google search, any social media, sponsorships of any kind including charitable support.

    A. Yes = 10 points
    B. No = 5 points

6. How much do you spend on marketing per year? This should include all printing, recruitment ads or human resource spending, your website, any digital ads, any type of sponsorship – charitable or otherwise, social media, along with traditional media like newspaper, radio, direct mail, and shared mail like Val Pak or money mailer.

    A. $10k or less = 1 point
    B. $10 – 25k = 6 points
    C. $25 – 50k = 8 points
    D. $50k plus = 10 points

7. Which option best describes what you feel is your unique selling point in the marketplace? Trying to help you understand the importance of a unique selling point to stand out from your national competitors who have more resources than you.

    A. In our ads, on our website, and anywhere we can mention that we are family owned, or locally owned, or how long we've been in business. We feel like one or all these features makes us stand out amongst our local and national competition, and that our customers also care about it. = 5 points

B. We have a truly unique selling point, it would compare to one of the most effective and famous examples from Domino's Pizza: Hot, fresh pizza to your door in 30 minutes or less or it's free. = 2 points

C. We don't need a Unique Selling Point in our industry. = 2 points

D. We could use some help crafting our Unique Selling Point. = 8 points

8. Do you make any pro-active efforts to recruit talent from the Ball State Community? Finding and keeping good talent is difficult today. Ball State alumni, students, and recent graduates are an abundant resource right in your back yard. Are you taking advantage of it?

A. Yes, we attend job fairs. = 7 points

B. We could benefit from recruiting more Ball State Students but haven't had the time to develop a plan or act yet. = 8 points

C. No, we have no need to recruit students, graduates or alumni of Ball State University. = 1 point

9. Choose the answer that best describes the success you are having with your current advertising and marketing

efforts. Most business owners and decision makers are busy, and it's easy to lose track of what's working, and not working.

    A. I know it works but we don't measure it. = 10 points
    B. Sometimes people tell us they heard or saw our ad somewhere. = 15 points
    C. We track every call, every lead, every conversion either manually or through our CRM. = 5 points
    D. Not sure it works; I keep spending money because we have a good relationship with the sales reps. = 20 points

10. How would you describe your social media strategy?

    A. We don't invest in social media = 5 points
    B. We hire a third party to create and manage our social media content. = 10 points
    C. We do it ourselves when we have time but could use some help in this area. = 20 points

11. Estimate how much of your business comes from the Ball State Community – directly or indirectly? Be honest here, if you operate a business in this region, and the largest economic driver is BSU, chances are your customers are in some way connected.

    A. Some, not sure how much exactly, but Ball State impacts us in some way either directly or indirectly. = 5 points

   B. At least one third or more of our business is a result of the university being here. = 8 points

   C. We are entirely dependent on the University for our sales. = 10 points

   D. Minimal to none – somehow, we operate a business in a college town and aren't impacted in any way. = 0 points

12. Could your business benefit by winning more business from the Ball State Community?

   A. Yes, 100%, I recognize the value of this community, and I need to adjust my marketing to directly target it. = 10 points

   B. No, we already have enough business from the Ball State Community, and we are unable to grow anymore. = 0 points

13. What answer below best describes how you fell about growing your business?

   A. Committed to investing in growth. = 10 points

   B. I'm the last generation, and we will either sell the business or close it down when I retire. = 0 points

   C. We are a branch of a corporation, or a franchise, and marketing decisions are managed by the corporate office. But they do listen to our valuable local feedback. = 7 points

   D. We're happy with our current level of sales and profits. = 0 points

14. Could you benefit from entertaining family, friends, clients, and employees at the only NCAA Division 1 sporting events in the region?

   A. Yes! = 8 points
   B. No, hospitality is not something I need in my business. = 0 points

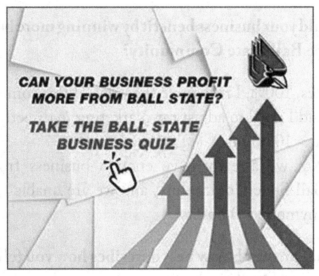

This is a digital display ad I run on our website promoting the quiz.

Chapter Fourteen

How I Advertise My Lead Magnets

There are **THREE** important things you need to attract prospects – successfully – using lead magnets.

First and most important is the content, or bait. Without good bait, you won't catch any fish. So, before you spend any money on advertising, commit to creating something your prospects will consider valuable, or at least interesting.

I spent a lot of time uncovering pain points pertaining to sponsorship with Ball State Athletics in Muncie. And as a result, the response to my lead magnets *exceeded my expectations* because they were educational and helpful.

I did nothing special, just adapted good ideas working elsewhere to my own situation, and this effort has delivered a higher return on investment than me making a bunch of random cold calls.

The best news … a good lead magnet … just like a good fishing lure … can be used and re-purposed many times.

And, unlike a fishing lure, you probably won't lose your lead magnet in a tree!

Second, you need a way to capture contact information, and ideally, an automatic way of sharing your lead magnet content with interested prospects.

I use software from **ClickFunnels** providing me with templated landing pages that automate the entire process of collecting leads and sharing my educational information.

I created a vanity URL, or a website address that's easy to remember that I promote in all my advertising.

My vanity URL is: **www.ballstatesports.com/profit**.

And when, for example, I run radio ads I can say, *"visit Ball State sports dot com slash profit to learn more"*.

When prospects visit **ballstatesports.com/profit** they are re-directed to my landing page where they can download the guide, take the quiz, or contact me directly.

The **third part** is *advertising your* lead magnet.

How will you get the word out? An even better question: How will you let the *right people* know – your ideal target customers?

When it comes to B2B marketing, there's good and bad news. The good news is most of what you are competing against is branding with no compelling reason for anyone to respond. This means direct-response ads (like the Fisher Investments ad from Chapter 9), and the type I'm encouraging you to use, will stand out in this branding environment.

The bad news is, there are fewer affordable media options

for B2B marketers. There are national business print and digital publications like *Forbes* or *Bloomberg Businessweek*, and others.

Most major cities have a business journal or some kind of local business publication. If you target a specific industry, their trade publications and newsletters are good places to advertise. You can also likely rent their subscriber mailing lists for direct mail marketing.

There are radio and television programs that work too. For example, *Fox News* and conservative media in general are proven to reach business owners. If you have a strong local talk-radio station, or can access Fox News affordably on cable TV, these are target-rich environments.

But most B2B advertising choices are not affordable to a purely local advertiser like me. In smaller cities, like Muncie, my options are even more limited.

So, with those challenges, in the next few chapters I will describe the local advertising methods I used to promote my lead magnets along with my results.

Thank you for your interest in becoming a corporate partner of Ball State Athletics.

If you would like to connect immediately, please email me:

Shane.nichols@
ballstatesportsproperties.com

Or - consider this:

I offer TWO educational resources so you can learn more about sponsorship without having to meet with or speak to anybody.

Do the research on your own, in the comfort of your office or home.

TAKE THE BALL STATE BIZ QUIZ.

It's a quick 14-question assessment designed to score your ability to profit from the Ball State Community.

Take the Ball State Biz Quiz By Clicking On This Button

OR:

This is the top half of my landing page, offering access to my guide or a link to the quiz.

Download our helpful, informative guide:

How Your Business Can Profit from an NCAA Sports Sponsorship

This is our 7th edition!

Find out how you can get a measurable return on ANY sports marketing/sponsorship investment - particularly at Ball State.

*This is the bottom half of the landing page,
where a prospect can submit their email address
and gain instant access to my guide.*

Congratulations for wanting to GROW your business!

The Download Link Is Ready for You...

Click the Button Below to Safely Gain Instant Access to Read and Download. GO CARDS!

Once someone submits their contact information, they are re-directed to a final step where they can access the download.

Chapter Fifteen

How to Win Over Other People's Clients

O nce you know who your ideal prospect is, the question you must ask is:

Who already has a relationship with them?

And how can you partner with them so they can introduce you as a trusted solution? It's kind of like a referral, but on a higher level because it's a *scaled referral*, reaching many at the same time.

This is one of the oldest marketing tactics in existence, finding a host, or joint venture partner, who can quickly (and affordably) introduce your product/service/offer in a credible way to *their* customers or members.

One of the most overlooked and undervalued groups offering this opportunity is your local Chamber of

Commerce. <u>Just being a member and listed in their directory can generate leads</u>.

But the real opportunity comes when you *activate* your membership by marketing your lead magnets and other offers to their membership.

Muncie has a strong chamber with over 500 members. Most of my existing sponsors are members, so the remaining members are good prospects worthy of a marketing investment.

I'm lucky because the chamber is also interested in the marketing and hospitality opportunities I offer through Ball State Athletics. I can trade my product and service, saving me money, in exchange for sponsoring their events, access to their membership mailing list, sending email blasts to their entire membership, and having ads in their week e-newsletter.

Even if you don't have a product or service to barter, *it's still worth the modest membership investment to be a member* to get your messaging in front of their entire membership.

Sponsored Email Blasts

One of my favorite marketing tactics is sending a dedicated email blast to all chamber members. Any day I choose the chamber will send a sponsored email blast to their entire membership featuring only my content.

And because the email is coming from them (a trusted source) and not from me (a salesperson) as a cold email, more people read them.

So, I hired a graphic designer to create a variety of email

blasts promoting my lead magnets. Then I schedule them to run at strategic times of the year that align with my sponsorship selling efforts.

And surprisingly I got an immediate response. On average, five prospects responded to my first series of email blasts promoting my lead magnets.

Another thing, my warm prospects also noticed my marketing. It helped me move them further along the sales process, without any labor from me.

Another benefit: The people I worked for in athletics noticed and were impressed by my pro-active effort.

Some prospects would email me, or call me, others would click on the email blast, arrive at my landing page, where I'd capture their contact information and then follow up.

I also tested this effort with other chambers in surrounding counties and at one point I had email blasts running with three different chambers – all using the same ads, promoting my lead magnets.

A word of warning about chamber email blasts: like all things when it comes to advertising, your response when repeatedly offering the same ad to the same group of people will eventually trickle to zero, especially if you operate in a smaller city like Muncie.

You can combat this in a few ways. First, by changing *how* you present your offers – by creating new ads, hooks and sales angles. Or by changing what media you approach the membership. For example, after running several weeks of email blasts, I would send letters in the mail promoting the same message.

One of my most successful email blast sales angles

was a warning about a company who sold fake Ball State football and basketball schedule calendars. This company would target college towns with aggressive telemarketing and mislead advertisers into believing their advertising was supporting Ball State Athletics.

So, I sent a few dedicated email blasts *warning* chamber members of this scam, and if they had already purchased a package, I would give them a free ad in our OFFICIAL football or basketball program.

This generated a huge response, and it went viral as members shared it with other friends, AND I turned a few of these advertising *victims* into new sponsors.

Some chambers may not allow you to send email blasts as often as you like. That's ok, they're just protecting their members from getting too many ads. It's good for you because their protection means higher readership.

A complement to sending email blasts can be running display ads in a chamber's own email newsletter. I run a display ad in their weekly email newsletter to members all year long, and I send the dedicated email blasts only during my peak selling season.

Other Chamber Marketing Opportunities: *A Special Offer for Members Only:*

Remember in Chapter 10 when I said whoever can spend the most money getting the attention of prospects wins?

One idea I've tested was to offer to pay for any new sponsor's chamber membership. This could cost me up to

$500 per prospect, but there are a lot of cool things having an offer like this can do for me:

1. It instantly sets my offer apart from all other B2B marketing competitors.
2. It adds credibility to me and my offer.
3. It offers something of clear value to my prospects – a free membership.
4. It incentivizes the chamber to help me market this offer – we both win!
5. It can be used as an incentive for an existing sponsor to renew and spend more.
6. To make the math work, I required a long-term commitment and a minimum investment level.

Golf Outings:

Every chamber has a golf outing; some are better than others. The good ones have huge participation and boast opportunities to interact with all the golfers through an array of sponsorships.

My favorite is to sponsor a hole, then create a fun activity for the golfers while they wait to tee off. This is a great way to meet hundreds of potential prospects, and they all come to you! It's important when networking like this to obtain everyone's contact information and then follow up by sending helpful educational information (links to your lead magnets).

Networking and Other Events:

The Muncie Chamber hosts networking events, featured speaker events, a luncheon series, community awards ceremonies, and more. Many of these are part of your membership; some allow you to have a booth like at a trade show.

Print Publications:

Most chambers distribute some type of print publication each year; these are great places to promote your lead magnets.

Create Your Own Event:

Many chambers are starving for valuable content or experiences they can share with their members, especially in smaller markets. You can propose an educational seminar, series, or luncheon focused entirely on providing value to their membership—you can in essence create your own event, further positioning yourself as an authority figure.

I encourage you to connect with your local chamber. For most B2B sellers, if harnessed correctly, it can be a source of all the prospects you'll ever need to hit your sales goals and maximize your earnings.

Dear Fellow Chamber Members,

Please be aware that a company called Prestige Marketing (sometimes they call themselves Elite Marketing) is trying to sell an advertising package that includes radio advertising and an unofficial Ball State Football schedule calendar.

This company is in no way affiliated with or has approval to use the name and likeness of Ball State Athletics, yet they continue to mislead local business owners with aggressive telemarketing efforts. And they do this in several markets, not just in Muncie.

I would advise you not to buy anything from them, and their advertising package won't get enough distribution to offer any real marketing value.

If you have already purchased a spot, and can't get your money back, please email me and I will provide you with a FREE AD in our upcoming 2022-23 Official Ball State Football Yearbook, distributed digitally on our official athletics website, and to all fans who attend games this fall.

This was the email blast warning about the fake calendar company, this got a huge response because it was newsworthy and offered something of value.

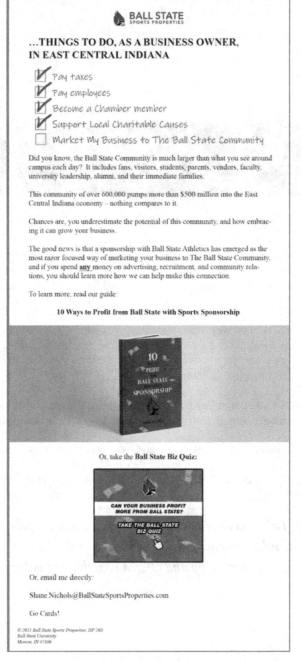

BALL STATE SPORTS PROPERTIES

...THINGS TO DO, AS A BUSINESS OWNER, IN EAST CENTRAL INDIANA

- ☑ Pay taxes
- ☑ Pay employees
- ☑ Become a Chamber member
- ☑ Support Local Charitable Causes
- ☐ Market My Business to The Ball State Community

Did you know, the Ball State Community is much larger than what you see around campus each day? It includes fans, visitors, students, parents, vendors, faculty, university leadership, alumni, and their immediate families.

This community of over 600,000 pumps more than $500 million into the East Central Indiana economy – nothing compares to it.

Chances are, you underestimate the potential of this community, and how embracing it can grow your business.

The good news is that a sponsorship with Ball State Athletics has emerged as the most razor focused way of marketing your business to The Ball State Community, and if you spend **any** money on advertising, recruitment, and community relations, you should learn more how we can help make this connection.

To learn more, read our guide:

10 Ways to Profit from Ball State with Sports Sponsorship

Or, take the **Ball State Biz Quiz**:

CAN YOUR BUSINESS PROFIT MORE FROM BALL STATE?

TAKE THE BALL STATE BIZ QUIZ

Or, email me directly:

Shane.Nichols@BallStateSportsProperties.com

Go Cards!

© 2021 Ball State Sports Properties. HP 260.
Ball State University
Muncie, IN 47306

This was the first dedicated chamber email blast I ran, and it performed very well capturing several leads.

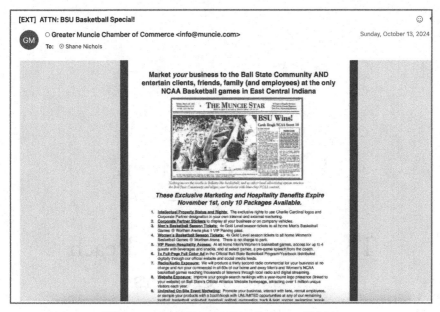

*This was a dedicated chamber email blast
promoting a basketball opportunity.*

*This is an example of a display ad I run in the
chamber's weekly email newsletter to their members.*

Chapter Sixteen

The Secret Weapon to Reach Business Owners

What's the secret weapon?

Send a letter. That's right, a good old-fashioned letter in the mail, inside an envelope, with a stamp. Because when you make this effort and invest this tiny sum – it costs less than $2 per prospect – it gives you the right to follow up.

VERY FEW other salespeople will take the time to do this. But they will all send emails, LinkedIn messages, try calling your prospect on their cell phones, even worse, texting them! Or, call your prospect's busy office during peak hours or stop by unannounced.

You – can let the post office do the manual labor for you. A few days after you send a letter, it will arrive, along with some other mail. *You just went from competing with hundreds of emails to 3 or 4 pieces of mail.* Your letter likely landed on your prospect's desk – their inner sanctum. Your letter will get opened because it looks personal, and it will satisfy their curiosity. When they read about your offer to educate them, it will make a real impression. And when you follow up, with an email a day or two later, the subject line of your email will refer to your letter ... vastly increasing the likelihood of getting a response ... and an appointment.

Mailing sales letters, in my experience, has been the most effective way to break through with busy decision makers. **Nothing** breaks through the clutter better than a piece of personalized mail your prospect must physically engage with.

Remember ... Your best prospects are hard-to-reach, time-starved, and overwhelmed by all things digital — especially email.

They value their time, and therefore, will ignore unsolicited calls from strangers at their office, and especially on their cell phones.

They may listen to your voicemail, then hit the delete button before hearing the first sentence out of your mouth.

And if you think *texting* them might work, think again. How do you like unsolicited texts from strangers? If you're like me, probably not well.

And if you take nothing else from this book, realize you can warm up ANY prospect <u>AND TRIPLE your chances of landing appointments</u> by mailing a simple sales letter before you call or email them.

A letter with persuasive copy, a compelling offer, sent to a curated list of prospects, then sent in sequence (more on that later) has routinely generated a 3% (and higher) response for me. **And what I mean by response is the prospect is reading my letters then contacting me!** In my sponsorship sales business, this 3% translates into *six figures* of potential lifetime customer value, all for the price of a stamp.

Whereas cold calling and cold emailing will yield, on average, a 1% (or less) response **and** take more of your manual labor, **and** you will have to physically experience *rejection after rejection after rejection* before finding that needle in a haystack.

The distinction between these two approaches is <u>how you value your physical and mental labor</u>. Think about that for a moment, and then imagine how each letter becomes your own little salesperson, *doing all the heavy lifting*, positioning you as someone worthy of your prospects' time, and magically setting you apart from the hundreds of other salespeople hounding them each day.

<u>Here is the most important benefit to direct mail:</u>

As you can tell by now, I believe cold calling and cold emailing – on their own – is a waste of your time trying to get the attention of cold targets.

BUT ... when you mail a letter to a cold prospect ... because you made *this personal gesture* ... because you invested time, money, and effort beyond a cold call or email when it was convenient to you ... it magically converts your effort from cold to warm, because now you have <u>earned</u> the right to:

FOLLOW-UP

If you want to show up where <u>none</u> of your competitors are, show up in the mailbox.

The largest digital B2B sellers on earth, like Google and Facebook, both <u>use direct mail</u> to reach business owners. They, too, realize there is a digital saturation point for connecting with overwhelmed prospects.

In this chapter I'll try to simplify what's needed to make direct mail work for you. The three key things to focus on are:

1. Your List
2. Your Delivery Method
3. Your Content

How to Build Mailing Lists of Your Best Prospects

The Muncie Chamber of Commerce has around 500 members, and members of a local chamber are often the most active and successful local businesses in any city – this list would be a great place to start for most B2B salespeople.

But I prefer compiling my own list. It takes more time, and effort, but I've had the most success focusing on about 100 **dream** targets *who spend money on exactly the type of thing I'm selling.*

In sponsorship sales, I target those who spend on radio, newspaper, billboard, digital advertising, and other sponsorships. I also target Alumni-owned businesses, and large vendors of our university.

If you live in a large metro area, subscribers and readers to the local business journal may be a good target. Most publishers rent their subscriber mailing list as another source of income, so don't be afraid to ask.

Or if you target a particular trade group, like HVAC business owners for example, you can rent a list of subscribers from their respective trade magazines.

One of my favorite resources for building lists (and researching a business for free) is Data Axle Reference Solutions, formerly Reference USA, and it's available online with a membership at your local library.

Data Axle Reference Solutions can help you build a mailing list or use it to research prospects based on a variety of criteria and search options.

I'm sure you're aware of companies like ZoomInfo, who provide contact information for thousands of companies – for a fee. A ZoomInfo subscription is a worthwhile investment and probably the best way to find a prospect's email address.

But I prefer Data Axle because it's easier to navigate, it's free, and based on a variety of data like the Yellow Pages, White Pages, annual reports, government data, business magazines, the US Postal Service, and the US Census Bureau.

You can search for businesses by company name, executive title, business type (industry group/SIC codes), geography, number of employees, sales volume, ownership structure, and other financial data.

When I began selling sponsorships for Ball State Athletics, I wanted to target businesses with at least $1M in gross sales with local ownership.

A quick search produced 456 results, and then I was able to download a spreadsheet with the name of the owner/president, mailing address, phone number, and about 25% of the time, also included the owners email address!

I found 456 prospects that met my criteria using Data Axle Reference Solutions for free through my local library

I then drilled this list down to who I determined were actively spending money on marketing, leaving me with about 100 viable prospects worth mailing to.

I then called each business to verify the contact information (including spelling of names), and their address information. This is important because each letter will cost up to $2 in handling, paper, and postage. You don't want to waste money sending mail to the wrong people, or wrong addresses.

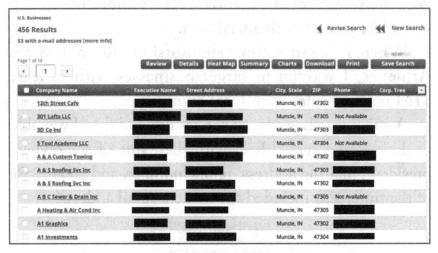

These are the results of my search for perfect prospects that I can download into an Excel spreadsheet, in some cases it includes the email addresses of the owner.

In the world of direct mail, the topic of lists goes deep, but most B2B sellers can prosper by focusing on a smaller curated list of dream prospects then relentlessly and creatively marketing to those folks. Don't overthink it.

The Delivery: How to Get Your Letters Opened, and Read

The kind of mail I'm urging you to send to business owners is <u>not</u> the impersonal, bulk-postage crap most people think of when they hear the term direct mail. I'm sure you get this type of mail at home, and I'm also betting you throw away 99.9% of it.

What I've learned about direct mail, from other B2B marketers, from hundreds of books, seminars, webinars, and by my own trial and error, is to adopt a much more personalized approach.

Just as in cold calling or cold emailing, we should know the person we are targeting, and if possible, *we begin the letter using their first name (Dear John) and hand-write their first and last name on the envelope.*

Your envelope should also include a local return address, so your prospect knows it's coming from a real person, adding more credibility.

An example of a real letter I mailed looking as personalized as possible.

I urge you to use First-Class postage, ensuring delivery in a timely manner – typically 2-3 days. Yes, it's more expensive than bulk mail postage, *but we've already agreed to invest money in getting the attention of our prospects because of the potential high return on investment.*

Sometimes I use FedEx, or the U.S. Postal Service's version of FedEx – Priority Mail. Both are delivered fast, offer tracking and confirmation of delivery – so you know when to follow up, and **it virtually guarantees your message bypasses gatekeepers and goes directly to your prospect**. I also strongly urge you to use *live* or real stamps you place on an envelope. I like to use commemorative stamps to attract even more attention.

And finally, to make certain our prospects don't miss out on our efforts, I send not one, but *a series of letters*. This is called *sequencing*, yet another tactic I learned from Dan Kennedy in his books *Magnetic Marketing* and *The Ultimate Sales Letter*.

Because I work in sports, I like to use sports themed stamps.
Here are examples from the USPS of "ball" themed stamps.

Kennedy noticed collection agencies never send just one letter. They send a series of letters (usually three), and in addition to the letters, sometimes they sprinkle in a few phone calls. And by the third letter, often stamped in red ink with **Final Notice,** <u>people usually respond</u>.

So that's how I ran my early direct mail campaigns. I took the same content from my *10 Ways to Profit* guide and repurposed it into a sales letter. Then I started sending sequenced campaigns, which you can view an example of in the following pages.

Another trick to get cold prospects to open my letters is to enclose a promotional item to make the envelope *feel lumpy* and more intriguing. Remember as a kid, when you'd get holiday cards from your grandma? And you could just tell by the feel of the envelope there was cash or a check inside? Same concept applies here – by including some type of promotional item in your mailings – something people can feel or see from the outside of the envelope – the more likely your letter will get opened out of simple curiosity.

For example, in addition to my letter, one time I printed a fake game ticket that served as a coupon for $500 off any sponsorship, which I stapled to each letter, making the envelope feel lumpy, and arousing curiosity.

This is an actual game-day ticket only we printed a coupon message on there for $500 off any new sponsorship.

To summarize this effort, we are very much coordinating a campaign over several weeks or even months, sending a series of letters first and following up later with email and phone calls.

Another point I'd like to make. This will seem like a lot of work, but please understand most of it can be outsourced to a direct mail firm.

You can hire someone to write a sales letter, to personally address envelopes, affix live stamps, and mail to your list.

About the only thing you must do, in my opinion, manually, is spend the time determining **who to mail to** – the curation of the list is worth the time and effort of doing it yourself.

Here is a specific example of one of my first campaigns applying these tactics on the following pages.

- **Letter #1:** I sent a personalized, one-page sales letter in a #10 envelope along with the game- ticket coupon as my promotional item, making the letter feel a bit lumpy, and intriguing.

Jeff, how can 70 + *of the most successful businesses in East Central Indiana* ALL BE WRONG?

May 15th, 2023

Jeff Client
Business
Address
Address

Dear Jeff,

You are receiving this letter because I've identified **YOU** as someone who spends their hard-earned PROFITS on *marketing* in East Central Indiana, and I believe … in fact, *I don't just believe*, **I KNOW** you could GREATLY BENEFIT by shifting just some of those dollars – NOT ALL OF THEM – just some of them, towards targeting (and profiting) from the Ball State Community.

My name is Shane Nichols, I grew up in nearby Marion, I graduated from Ball State University, and for the past six years I've been in charge of selling corporate sponsorships for Ball State Athletics. I've spent my entire life in advertising, **both as a seller and buyer**, giving me an OBJECTIVE perspective, one you can benefit from – for free. I've also published 2 books on local marketing (search my name on Amazon) *and my lifetime of experience has led me to these conclusions*:

There are 3 undisputed FACTS you should seriously consider as a business owner/marketer in this region:

1. Local traditional media (like the newspaper, local radio, cable TV, and others) for a variety of reasons (I'm sure you notice through your own personal media habits) *are no longer as dominant, important, or as effective as they used to be*. What's puzzling is they all reach fewer and fewer people, AND they've become more expensive!
2. Muncie is **lucky**. Lucky because we have Ball State University. Believe me when I say this, because I compare Marion (where I grew up) to Muncie, their economy isn't even close to Muncie's. Even with Indiana Wesleyan's growth (a great school), it's STILL not even close. At the end of this letter, you can gain access to educational resources (supported by independent research) detailing how much Ball State impacts our region's economy, *but the easiest comparison I can make* … it's like Muncie hosting *not one*, **but two Superbowl's each year**. And this is not an exaggeration.
3. Google, Facebook, and other new whiz-bang digital media *aren't the answer*. If nothing else, the proliferation of social and digital media has made everything more fragmented, **and confusing**. Bottom line is nothing reaches the Ball State Community more effectively, and efficiently than what I can offer you … a comprehensive, customized presence through *sports marketing and hospitality*.

So, What's in It For YOU, Jeff?

As a business owner, please tell me what possible reason, regardless of the type of business you operate, whether it's a business who sells to other businesses (B2B), or one who sells to

1

- **Letter #2:** About 10 days later, a second letter arrives. But at the top is a red stamp that says, *Second Notice*. The lumpy item I inserted for this letter was one-half of our official corporate partner stickers, I then reference why I sent only ½ of a sticker in the letter.

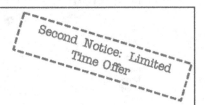

Late May of 2023
(Perfect Bird Weather)
FROM THE DESK OF:
Charles A. Cardinal
Official Mascot of Ball State
Athletics

Hey Jeff, Why Did I Send You Half a Sticker?

Dear Jeff,

Enclosed is **one half of a very special sticker**, I only sent you HALF for two reasons — ONE ... I wanted to get your attention.

Two ... I wanted to (hopefully) open your eyes to one of the greatest benefits of sports sponsorship — and that is the ability to use our logos and images in your own advertising — helping you appeal to our affluent fans and distinguishing you from your local and national competitors. Sounds intriguing right?!

About two weeks ago our guy in charge of sponsorship — Shane Nichols — sent you a letter with our BEST EVER offer to becoming a sponsor. Please forgive him for being SOOOOOOO

Please turn to page 2

1

- **Letter #3:** About 10 days later, a third letter arrives. At the top of the letter and on the envelope, it now says, 3rd or *Final Notice*. I didn't use a lumpy item in this letter, instead I offered to pay their chamber membership if they become a sponsor.

Early June of 2023

Ike Mendoza
CINTAS
1234 1234
Muncie, IN 47305

BALL STATE
UNIVERSITY

Ike, Find Out How YOU Can Get Up To $500 towards your Chamber Membership, *On us!*

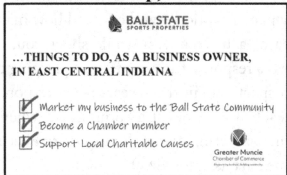

Greetings Ike,

By now you've received a letter from me, AND from our famous mascot Charlie Cardinal. We've not heard back from you – YET– but no worries, I wanted to share *another* benefit only for <u>NEW SPONSORS</u>!

We are big fans of our local chamber. **The Greater Muncie Chamber of Commerce** counts over 700 members and is the largest chamber in the region.

Please turn over to next page   1

You might be wondering, how well did this work? About a dozen clients responded to my first sequenced campaign, allowing me to hit my sales goal, and providing six-figures worth of lifetime value. If I had the time to follow up with a phone call to each prospect who received all three letters, I would have booked even more appointments. I got the most responses on the second and third letter.

You may be thinking: *Isn't this overkill, Shane?*

Absolutely not. This is the kind of persistence and repetition needed for marketing to work.

Try paying attention for one week to how often you see or hear a GEICO or Progressive Insurance ad. They are some of the most prolific marketers on earth. I'd bet – if you really paid attention – and counted how many ads you saw or heard each week … it would shock you.

Below is a response from my first sequencing campaign, from a prospect who in three years never responded to any cold outreach. I consider it a compliment when someone refers to my marketing materials as *aggressive* (as if emailing all the time isn't as aggressive).

The difference is printed mail has more impact than any other tactic when trying to engage with cold prospects.

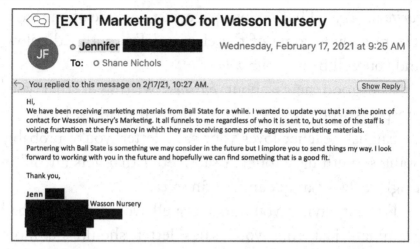

This email was sent to me after this business received 3 different letters in the mail. They continue to be a prospect I stay in touch with, and eventually have a good chance of selling them a sponsorship.

It's easy to delete emails and voicemails. But it takes more effort to ignore a personally addressed piece of mail and then throw it away. Curiosity is in your favor when you use the mail correctly.

How to Write Sales Letters That Generate a Response

Not a writer? Hate to write? Good news, <u>you can hire someone else</u>, or even better, **copy what others are doing for FREE!**

Better news, writing a sales letter is easier than you think. If you created a lead magnet, like a guide or a quiz, you could repurpose a lot of that information into a sales letter. My first few sales letters were just shorter versions of my *How to Profit* guide.

How long does your letter need to be? For starters, *just*

write one page. That's it, one page, just one side of one page. Try to include some of the elements I've outlined below, and you will be on your way.

The good news about *business* writing is that your prospects won't respond to intellectual writing. In fact, if an English teacher loves your sales letter, you're probably doing something wrong! A sales letter that gets an "F" in English class can get an "A+" in sales.

I'm not saying you can misspell words and use bad grammar, just that your sales letter should be more conversational where getting your point across is more important. And the point you're trying to get across is that *you are a provider of cutting-edge educational trends in their industry, and they will learn something if they meet with you.* Nothing more.

To break it down in simplest terms, you want to accomplish these three things:

A. **Identify their problem** – *When selling sponsorships, the problem I'm trying to solve is how to help local business owners profit more from the gigantic economic force of Ball State University.*

B. **Agitate the problem a bit** – On the next few pages is one of my actual letters. *Notice how I'm challenging prospects to wake up and realize the vast amount of potential if they just start catering to the affluent audience, I call the Ball State Community.* I'm purposely trying to stimulate emotion!

C. **Provide a solution** – *The solution I lay out, above all other options for marketing to the Ball State Community,* *is my elevator pitch that sponsorship is the most efficient and effective solution, with proof.*

Instead of telling you in words what makes up a successful sales letter, I'd rather show you one of my letters that got a good response. Don't be intimidated by its length; this letter is the culmination of every letter I've written in 7 years selling sponsorships. All you need to do is start with one page!

Here I point out 15 features I try to include in every sales letter; these are time-tested, proven, direct-response copy techniques that have worked forever. And will continue to work if you apply them in your own communications to cold prospects.

1. **Headline**: This can be at the top of the page and centered, or just below the address line after the Dear ....
2. **A photo or image** to grab attention somewhere at the top of the letter.
3. **Elevator Pitch**: How you help your clients do/get better, cheaper, faster, even in worst-case scenarios.
4. Use **Subheads**. Subheads are just mini headlines interspersed throughout your letter to help break up the uniformity, and to create a different readership path. Some people will only skim rather than read the letter word for word, and the subheads should give them an easy summary of the letter's intent.

Please Don't Read This Letter if You Are Not Planning to
Grow or Stay in Business Here In Muncie

March 7th, 2022

Lehman's Inc

Muncie, IN 47302

Dear John,

| | #1 Headlines |
| #2 Photo |

Would You Ignore The Super Bowl If It Were Played Here In Muncie?

#3 Elevator Pitch

Hello, my name is Shane Nichols, and I'm in charge of developing corporate sponsorship for Ball State Athletics.

I help business owners (like you) **profit** from the Ball State Community, the largest most affluent economic force in the entire region. And I can do this (for you) more efficiently and effectively than any other form of advertising. Saving you a lot of time, hassle, and valuable cash.

Just WHO is the Ball State Community?   #4 Subhead

Our community should be of great interest to you, regardless of what type of business you operate. It's bigger than most realize, with unmatched spending power … and includes **students** on campus, their **visiting parents & friends**, plus the **thousands who work on campus** (don't forget *their* families too) along with **university leaders** who control millions in spending.

It also includes a few hundred thousand **loyal alumni** who live around here, and along the I-69 corridor between Fort Wayne and Indianapolis – *who also visit, who also make buying decisions for their respective businesses and personal lives.* And don't forget the hundreds of thousands of **educational visitors** coming to campus for a variety of reasons, and the hundreds of thousands of **sports fans** who attend our sporting events each year (also a few hundred busloads of **visiting teams**).

I graduated from Ball State in 1996, I grew up in nearby Marion, I've spent 20 + years in advertising, published two books on marketing, and over the past 4 seasons representing Ball State Athletics, **I have developed a very strong belief as it pertains to doing business here:**

Turn Over to Page 2

1

5. **Hooks, and Selling Angles.**
6. **Identify the most common objections.**

If you operate a business here, whether you sell to consumers (B2C) or other businesses (B2B) – and if you want to continue to grow, prosper and profit here – then you should be *actively wooing* the Ball State Community

Table 2, Economic Impact of Ball State University

Category	Delaware County	East Central Indiana	Indiana
Total Employment	10,074	11,843	13,613
Private Non-Farm Employment	5,754	6,765	7,776
Gross Domestic Product ($1,000's)	433,640	509,820	586,000
Personal Income ($1,000's)	361,120	424,560	488,000
Resident Population	23,976	28,188	32,400
Ball State Student Population	18,000	20,000	21,500

This graph comes from a study authored by the distinguished professor of economics, Michael Hicks. If you would like a complete copy emailed to you, just let me know, my email is at the end of this letter.

Would you ignore the Super Bowl if it were being played here in Muncie? As you know, Super Bowl's pump massive amounts of money into their host cities. Last I checked, it was around $250 million per game. Imagine (if for some crazy reason) the NFL staged *not one*, BUT TWO Super Bowls in Muncie – **in the same year?**

When you choose to ignore the Ball State Community, you are ignoring the equivalent of TWO Super Bowls' worth of economic potential

Frankly, I am puzzled as to why more business owners haven't come to this same realization. I've encountered many who cling to self-limiting grudges against the university (or athletics) for a variety of reasons. One business owner complained he'd lost numerous bids for the University's business and didn't think the bidding process was fair. Here's my advice, **the real profit is in THE COMMUNITY, not the University.** Unless you construct large buildings worth millions of dollars, you can make gobs more money catering to our community (*which happens to include thousands of business owners*) rather than winning bids from a state-supported bureaucracy. Another objection I hear a lot is:

> #6 Identify Objections

"But my other advertising already reaches the Ball State Community?"

> #5 Selling Angles

Turn to Page 3

2

7. What Benefit Justifies the Cost?
8. Where does the money come from for this, and what other expense am I cutting to pay for this?

Look, I'm not going to bash other media, I believe all media work to some degree. But I can prove to you that *local traditional media simply doesn't reach our community like it used to.* Just look at what's happened to the newspaper industry. If you spend money on local advertising, just realize that <u>our athletics marketing platform has emerged to become the most affordable, effective way to reach the Ball State Community</u>. And it's fun, this is sports after all.

As a savvy entrepreneur, I'm sure you've noticed the value of live sports **has exploded**. The NFL, NBA, PGA, NHL, and NCAA are all getting record amounts of money for the rights to their games. Why? Because live sports are *the only events we all still share together.* This used to be the case with TV, radio, and not too long ago – the newspaper.

But today, we all watch and listen to whatever we want, whenever we want. The only thing that brings us together anymore is live sporting events. And here is a secret about sports, they happen to be the best platform for reaching elusive, time-starved, **business owners**. *(Here's another secret very few realize, especially if you want to win business from the university itself, sponsorship is also the best way to reach* **university leaders and decision-makers**.*)*

| #5 Selling Angles | **Yes, You Can Afford This, And Here's How** |

There is a good chance you are spending money on something that isn't giving you a measurable return on investment – or any fun. This could be on subscriptions of some kind, digital or social marketing efforts, local traditional media, other sponsorships – THIS *is what I'm asking you to consider investing with me,* not additional spending. I'm simply asking you to reallocate your investments.

| #7 Justify Cost |

I'm asking you to be like Warren Buffett: Sell the losers, invest in the winners. By the way, he invests (indirectly through his conglomerate of companies) in *many* forms of sports sponsorship. Including his hometown Nebraska Cornhuskers.

The great thing about sports sponsorship is it's a tax-deductible business expense AND you can fund it from <u>4 different budgets</u>:

1. **Marketing/Advertising Budget**
2. **Community Relations** (charitable causes, local sports teams, the arts)
3. **Recruitment** (the armed forces are among our biggest clients, if it works for them, it can work for you)
4. **Hospitality/Entertainment** (tickets/VIP hospitality for clients, employees, your family!)

| #8 Where the $ Comes From |

Turn Over To Page 4   3

9. Who Else Is Doing it so your prospect can validate their judgment?

I'd bet you a good sum of money that if you just take five minutes to closely examine your current spending, *you will find room for improvement and optimization.* AND FUN!

You're probably wondering … what does it cost? Well, we customize every sponsorship to meet the needs of each client, but our minimum investment is only **$5,000 per year**. And … <u>billing can be spread across as many as 12 months to help with your cashflow!</u>

That's just $416 a month, a utility bill for some businesses??? I can even delay all billing until next year, imagine enjoying an entire football season as a partner, **and not paying a thing until 2023?**

#9 Who Else Is Doing This?

You Aren't Alone In Making This Wise Investment

Those who embrace the Ball State Community happen to be the most successful, innovative businesses in the region. Here are a few testimonials from some valued partners:

Community Hospital of Anderson, along with the entire Community Health Network are proud sponsors of Ball State Athletics. We recognize the powerful presence Ball State University has not only in East Central Indiana, but all along the I-69 corridor to Indianapolis and believe our sponsorship with athletics is among the most efficient ways of connecting to this community. **Leah Campbell, Director of Consumer Brand, Community Hospital of Anderson**

Ball State Online is excited to partner with Ball State Athletics. Ball State Online offers 100+ programs, 100% online. Most of our marketing efforts have focused on reaching specific audiences for specific academic programs. Since including Ball State Athletics in our marketing strategy, we were able to add an awareness component that we were previously lacking. **Craig Meinhart, Director of Marketing and Communications, Ball State Online and Strategic Learning**

Lehman's has been in business for over 90 years, and during that time Muncie has changed from industrial economy to one more reliant on the university and healthcare. We've adjusted our advertising accordingly, and we find one of the best ways to target the Ball State community is through our sponsorship with Athletics. **John Primmer, owner, Lehman's Heating and Cooling**

Mancino's has partnered with Ball State Athletics for many years. We feed athletes, students, faculty, and we provide food for their officials and press at all basketball games. Sponsorship gives us access to relationships and visibility I can't buy anywhere else. **Jeff Carrigan, Owner, Mancino's Pizza of Muncie**

"When Roots first opened, we worked with Shane's team and created a promotion to drive traffic to our restaurant. Whenever a Ball State Men's basketball opponent misses two free throws in a row, EVERY fan gets a free order of tater tots. It's been a great way to get new customers to try our restaurant, and when it happens during a game, the crowd goes crazy! **Scott Wise, Partner, Root's Restaurant Group**

Pepsi's partnership with Ball State Sports Properties has truly been a partnership – from both a business and personal perspective. Their team has been awesome to work with and are truly concerned about making our partnership a win-win for all involved. **Rick McClain, Workplace KAM, PepsiCo Northwest Division**

Pridemark Construction has been a longtime partner of Ball State Athletics. We support our student athletes through the Pridemark Construction Athlete of the Week, and local charities like the Youth Opportunity Center through hospitality, and sponsorship gives us exposure to decision makers on campus and in the community. **Mike Tschuor, President, Pridemark Construction**

See the next page for an exclusive first-time sponsor offer

4

10. **Make them a compelling offer** to try your product or service, perhaps a discount, or a free trial with a DEADLINE!

Can you at least admit you're already PASSIVELY benefiting from Ball State? Why not benefit *even more* by ACTIVELY seeking more profit from the Ball State Community?

So now, I'd like to make you an offer, it's first-time sponsors only, and I will give you this entire list of marketing and hospitality assets valued at $18,150 ... for just $5,000

#10 Make An Offer

1. **Football Season Tickets:** 4x Gold Level season tickets to all Men's Football Games ($1,300 value)
2. **VIP Parking Pass:** VIP Parking Pass for all Football games ($800 value)
3. **Basketball Season Tickets:** 4x Gold Level season tickets to all home Men's Basketball Games ($2,000 value)
4. **VIP Parking Pass:** VIP Parking Pass for all Men's basketball games ($800 value)
5. **Website Exposure:** Year-Round Logo Presence (with link to your website) on Ball State's Official Athletics Website ($2,500 value)

6. **Full Page Full Color Ad** in the Official Ball State Football Program ($3,000 value)
7. **Another Full-Page Full Color Ad** in the Official Ball State Basketball Program ($3,000)
8. **"Corporate Partner" Stickers** to display on your place of business or service vehicles
9. **Fan Jam Booth:** One free booth at our annual Fan Jam event held in August on the football field at Scheumann Stadium attracting thousands of fans who come tour our facilities and meet our athletes, coaches, and our sponsors. ($2,500 value)
10. **Partnership Announcement:** We will announce your partnership in social media posts on our official athletics Facebook and Twitter account, reaching over 75,000 followers. AND we will announce your partnership in our weekly Birdfeed email newsletter, reaching over 20,000 fans, season ticket holders, alumni, and many more. ($1500 value)
11. **Official Gear:** New sponsors get an official Nike Dry-Fit Half-Zip pullover – the same gear our coach's wear! ($250 value)
12. **Radio:** A LIVE read commercial announcing your partnership during a broadcast of Ball State Football on WLBC, or during a Men's and Women's Basketball Game on BLAKE and WERK-FM, your choice. ($500 value)

You see, I can <u>give you so much for so little</u> because we are good at turning first-time sponsors into *long-term partners*. Most of our clients have been with us for many years.

#7 Justify Cost

OBVIOSULY ... *I can only sell a handful of these special sponsorship packages.*

urn over to page 6 for the conclusion of this letter, and more! 5

11. Give a **reason** why you can make your special offer.

12. Don't forget to include a **DEADLINE!**

13. **Offer a guarantee**; find some way to reduce their risk.

14. Make it abundantly clear **how to respond and reach you.**

15. **Use a P.S.** to highlight your lead magnets or reinforce your offer.

#11 Reason Why?

You see, I can give you so much for so little because we are good at turning first-time sponsors into *long-term partners*. Most of our clients have been with us for many years.

#12 Deadline

Again, this offer expires on August 31st, 2022 – *If we haven't sold out by then – I promise you we will sell this out so act now!*

100% GUARANTEED
To reduce your risk of purchasing this package, if by the end of football season, you are not satisfied with our efforts to help you profit from your investment, *you can cancel during basketball season, and recoup half of your investment.*

Don't wait, here's how to reach us:

#13 Guarantee

1. Email: Shane.Nichols@BallStateSportsProperties.com
2. Phone: 317-679-6573 (this is my cell, text, or call)
3. Visit www.BallStateSports.com/Profit for free educational resources

#14 How to reach you

P.S. If this specific package does not suit your needs, challenge us to develop a customized presence to meet your specific marketing goals – I'm 100% confident of our abilities to make this happen!

#15 Use a P.S.

P.P.S. We offer two educational resources for prospective clients to learn more about sponsorship without having to meet with me or speak to me. First, I recommend scanning my 41-page guide *10 Ways to Profit from Ball State with Sports Sponsorship* featuring 10 different illustrations of local business owners profiting from their sponsorship with us. I also encourage you to take the *Ball State Biz Quiz*, to further see if you can benefit from the Ball State Community. You can email me, and I'll send a copy, or visit www.BallStateSports.com/Profit

6

P.S. Try This Trick ... *Mail* **Your Email**

If you won't jump on board with my direct mail strategy, at least try this trick. This works well for prospects you know are a perfect fit, someone you can help, but they haven't responded to any of your cold outreach attempts.

Print the last email you sent, one they haven't responded to, and attach a sticky note saying something like, *"I know you're busy, and get a lot of emails...I just wanted you to be sure you don't miss out on our offer to..."*.

Then print and send that email in an envelope, personally addressed to them, with a first-class stamp.

Even better, send it FedEx® or in a Priority Mail® envelope. This will cost a bit more, but it guarantees they open it, especially the FedEx option.

Then follow up with a phone call. This works exceptionally well for me – usually a prospect will respond out of sheer guilt. Often, they will call you!

Chapter Seventeen

The 10 Habits of Highly Effective Emailing for B2B Sales Professionals

Realize that email, and a calendar invite from your email account, is the #1 way of securing appointments with your prospects. In baseball, as the book *Moneyball* explained, the #1 stat Billy Beane relied on to determine a player's contribution to winning was their *On-Base-Percentage*.

In B2B selling, the #1 stat that determines your success is *Getting Appointments with Ideal Prospects*.

And getting better at writing emails is critical to landing more appointments. Also, being more strategic about how you email prospects will improve your response rate.

Emailing strangers one at a time ... out of the blue ... just like cold calling a prospect ... out of the blue ... whenever it suits your selfish goals and needs ... has become ... in my educated opinion ... a *complete waste of your valuable time* ... and your employer's resources.

So, what do you do?

You must provide a compelling reason to reply to your cold email.

If you've ever had salespeople emailing you, most of them say some form of this:

Hi, this is so and so, and we sell so and so, and it does all this great stuff; can we set up a time to meet so you can buy?

Without some personal connection or referral in your favor, assume a 1% response sending individual emails to prospects who don't know you.

So out of every 100 emails you send, you might get 1 appointment.

Do those seem like good odds?

Does that seem like a good use of your time?

If you are a sales manager or business owner, do you expect to grow and prosper with results like those?

I encourage you to adopt some time-tested email strategies I've learned from my 20+ years in B2B sales, and through hundreds of books and seminars from the most successful marketers on the planet.

The 10 Habits of Highly Effective B2B Cold Emailing

1. Determine WHO to email, and use their first name:

- You must know your prospects *first name* and use their name in every email. You would be surprised at how many emails are sent – impersonally – without using a prospect's first name.

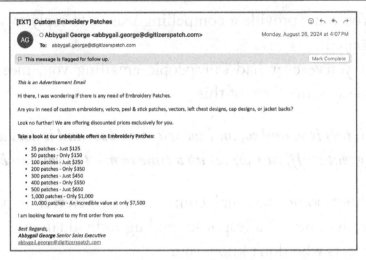

This cold email, from someone I've never heard of or met before, was not only impersonal but announced at the top this email is an advertisement!

- There is a company that sells training aids for pitchers who send me emails almost weekly. I don't buy anything for our baseball team. But somehow, I'm on their list – which I later learned has over 90,000 email addresses on it.

- I get emails all the time from people who not only fail to use my name, they also haven't done any research – because I'm not the buyer for what they are selling – yet they have wasted time/energy and money sending me their emails.

- In my NCAA sports sponsorship business, I want prospects who are spending money on advertising in my market and can afford my product. When I sold broadcast TV advertising, I wanted people with destination businesses (think car dealers) with high average sales, and a constant need for traffic/customers/sales and could afford a $10k per week spend.

- What are your ideal prospect characteristics?
- WHO is this person who buys for this ideal company? And use their first name when you email them.
- The person you are trying to get an appointment with should be the decision maker or influencer within that company spending money on exactly the type of thing you are selling.
- Don't be lazy – take time to develop a smaller curated list of great prospects rather than a massive list of OK targets.
- You always want to be working on 50-100 rock-solid, dream targets.
- There have never been more resources available at the tip of any salespersons fingers to uncover who makes decisions, and what their contact info is. Make an investment in one or more of these services, it's worth it: LinkedIn Sales Navigator, ZoomInfo, Data Axle (available free via the library), and often the corporate website will list the leadership and their contact information.

2. **Realize your subject line is just as important as what you say in your email:**

- What you read ... *anywhere* ... is determined by the strength of the headline, same principle applies here.

- The subject line in your email is like the headline to an article you read.
- When your email appears in a prospect's email inbox, they see your name, the subject line, and sometimes, a preview of your message.
- So, assume they can only see your name and about 5-8 words of your subject line. And in tiny type because most of our prospects are viewing email on their cell phones.
- The best subject/headlines do one (or more) of these 5 things:

1. Offer newsworthy info.
2. Arouse curiosity.
3. Appeal to self-interest.
4. Offer a benefit.
5. Are personal in nature – a friend, or a referral from a friend.

- **Idea starter: Personal + Newsworthy + Self Interest**
  o *Geoff, this is how AI can help you …*
  o *Geoff … "election-proof" your marketing*
- **Idea starter: Personal + Curiosity**
  o *How you can win at advertising, Geoff*
- **Idea starter: Personal + Self Interest**
  o *Never Waste $ Again, Geoff*
- **Idea starter: Mention Peer + Result**
  o *1ˢᵗ National Bank Just Hired Me, Geoff*
  o *Geoff, your friend Mike just hired me.*

- **Idea starter: Just make up something short and fun:**
  - *I Heart You Geoff*
  - *Me + You = Success*
  - *Free ice cream, pls open* (you better deliver on this promise if you use a gimmick like this!)
- **Idea starter from professional copywriter Neville Medhora: End result they want + Time period + Address the objections.**
  - *How to drive traffic + today + at no cost to you.*
  - *Entertain your customers + every week + with zero effort.*
  - *Stop wasting money + Immediately + on your local advertising.*
- **Another from Neville Medhora: Take this action + Specific Time Period + Result**
  - *Read this email + in 1 minute + Discover New Ideas*
  - *Open your mind + just for a minute + Find Freedom*
  - *Profit + Immediately + Just by reading my email.*

3. **You need to offer a BRIEF yet compelling hook or selling angle to increase the response rates to your cold emails:**

- Realize many of your prospects are reading your emails on a cell phone.
- Your first email should be short, to the point, and offer unique value.
- A hook or angle is simply some reason, device, or unique offer that gets the attention of your prospect.

- *Offering a free consultation is no longer compelling to most prospects, unless you are a medical doctor or lawyer.* This has become a tired, over-used and easily ignorable offer and will appeal to only a tiny percentage of prospects who are ready to buy today.
- You will get a much higher response (and tons more appointments) by appealing to the larger percentage of prospects who may be interested but are in the *learning phase.* They are willing to learn more, to be educated, but not *sold too* ... yet.
- The most effective thing you can offer a prospect, leading to the most possible appointments is offering to educate about the latest trends in their industry.
  - o It should be *Cutting Edge Research.* Create a compelling educational presentation like "**The Six Most Important Insights into XYZ**".
  - o Then, in your first email say something like ... "Hi Geoff, have you heard about this report?" (*No, he hasn't).* "Geoff, don't you want to be the type of executive who likes to be on the cutting edge of the most advanced trends in your industry?" (*Yes, he does).*
  - o This is a good enough email script alone to triple the response to your cold emails.
- Other ways to secure an appointment:
  - o A referral.
  - o A testimonial from a meaningful and recognizable peer.
  - o A demonstration – but this is getting tired and overused.

- Putting a combination of these sales angles and hooks is the most effective way of getting a response to your email.

4. DON'T use 3rd Party Software (like Mailchimp) for Cold Email Prospecting!

- Corporate security is a **_big deal_**, and a growing concern for every business.
- The future of email is *more* spam filters, meaning ... it's a waste of your time sending hundreds of emails (with weak copy) using some kind of software – to a large *cold* list.
- Lots of people send me cold emails trying to sell me stuff, and many use software (like Mailchimp) to make their job *seemingly* easier.
- Software generated emails (also known as 3rd party emails) *always* get caught up in corporate spam filters and aren't reaching your targets. Why? Because spam filters FLAG unknown senders who use 3rd party software.
- Email software should be used ONLY FOR RETENTION and ENGAGEMENT with EXISTING CLIENTS ... those who have *opted-in and agreed* to hear from you.
- Your emails should come directly from your business email account – Outlook, or Gmail. The person sending the email's address should be you@yourbusinessname.com.

- Since you're working from a smaller group of high value targets, it should be no issue to manually send your emails. Copy, pasty, send. Worth the effort.
- If you must send a mass email, I recommend using Mail-Merge via Microsoft Word and Outlook. This allows you to personally address everyone by their first name.
- There are similar plugins – or software tools – to do the same thing using Gmail.
- NEVER include this anywhere in your email: "To unsubscribe, click here" is admitting you're using some type of impersonal software and your prospect is not worth the time and effort to individually email. Newsflash – they didn't subscribe! This is a cold prospect!! To suggest they did subscribe *unknowingly* is even worse!

5. Commit to a Campaign vs. Sending Random Emails:

- Your email is competing against a TSUNAMI of clutter bombarding your prospect every day. You need to be prepared to send as many as 12 different communications using a variety of different media to reliably get the attention of your best prospects. **Email should be just one of many arrows in your quiver.**
- Combine email with direct mail, phone calls, LinkedIn messages, show interest in their social

media feeds, follow them, provide comments on their posts.

- A combined effort using multi-media with persuasive messaging to a curated list of worthy prospects is a strategic effort vs. random cold outreach.

- Remind yourself what an average sale is worth, what is the customer's lifetime value, and that should be all the motivation you need to invest in this type of effort.

- As I mentioned in the previous chapter, something I often do when I'm targeting a prospect is print one of my emails then mail it with a sticky note attached saying "I know you are busy, but I'm worth a moment of your time."

6. Your Cold Email Should be the Opposite of Decorative, It Should be ANALOG:

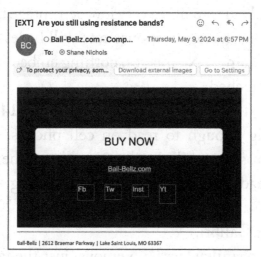

If you include pictures and links, they are blocked by spam filters and require your prospects approval to see. Not a good idea if you want your email read.

- When I say analog, I mean it should contain nothing fancy **but words**, maybe a link to an educational resource.
- The company I mentioned earlier – who sells training equipment to baseball players – sends me emails full of images, videos, and even worse – *buy buttons.* They are asking me to buy, and I don't even know who they are! Crazy, right? They must not think so. Because they continually embed snazzy pictures and videos in every email and each one gets blocked by my corporate spam filter. I've had to manually approve each email before it enters my email box.
- *Your email's ONLY JOB is to arouse interest, not make a sale.* These are cold prospects. You can make sales to warm prospects once they've opted into your email marketing, but trying to sell them cold via email is a very low percentage battle where your average response rate will be less than 1%.
- Again … No images, nothing embedded, nothing attached.
- Just use simple typed words in **14 pt type** – big enough to read on cell phones. Your older prospects will thank you, many of them must use reader-type glasses to read anything.
- Use an easy-to-read font like Times New Roman or Calibri.
- No smiley faces, no emojis, just the facts.
- If you want to share photos, or videos, use a link and make sure it's hosted in a safe trusted

environment by a recognized name – like Google Drive, Amazon Cloud etc.

7. **WHEN to Send Your Cold Emails for Better Response Rates:**

- I've learned a lot from the most successful tech companies like Salesforce, who operate in the ultra-competitive software business and have developed the most comprehensive, tested methods for finding and landing new clients.
- There is a great book I recommend any salesperson read about how Salesforce became who they are today: *Predictable Revenue: Turn Your Business Into a Sales Machine with the $100 Million Best Practices of Salesforce.com* by Aaron Ross and Marylou Tyler
- They sent most of their emails *before 9am or after 5pm*, avoiding Mondays and Fridays when most salespeople are emailing, even sending emails on the weekends.
- Technology allows for emails to be sent in the future, so schedule them to be sent early in the morning or …
- Late at night.
- Or on the weekend.
- These days: Tuesday, Wednesday, Thursday, Saturday, or Sunday.
- Never these days: Monday, or Friday.
- I send my cold emails at 7:11 in the morning using Outlook's schedule-send. So, most of my emails

arrive while I'm still in bed – yet my prospects think I'm working!

- Even sending emails to existing clients, I use this strategy. I want my communications to stand out from the rest.

8. Make It Easy to Connect.

- For most of us, email is about getting appointments.
- Once a prospect has shown interest, make it easy for your prospect to choose a time – give them 3 options of when you're available they can choose from. Eliminate the need to go back and forth.
- Offer multiple choice of times/dates for them to choose, then make it clear you will send an invite. Do the work for them.
- Provide a Calendly link (or similar software) if you prefer this automated way of scheduling.

9. Optimize your Signature Line with an offer!

> **Shane Nichols**
> **GM, Ball State Sports Properties**
> **See if your business can profit more from the Ball State Community ...**
> **Take the** *Ball State Biz Quiz*: BallStateSports.com/quiz
>
> **Book a discovery chat with me:**
> https://tidycal.com/shanenichols/30-minute-meeting

- Most people include a fancy signature line with their company logo, phone number, fax number, and other information that does not help you land more appointments.

- Instead, use this valuable space to offer something of value to your prospects. Offer a pitch to download something educational, offer a link to a video about how your solutions are unique, or a testimonial from peers in your industry. There are software companies (Terminus) that exist solely to capitalize on this often forgotten and underutilized space.

- Newsflash! They already have your email, no need to have it included in your signature line.

- As we discussed, <u>don't use your photo, or image or LOGO of any kind</u>. A lot of people include their photo, **don't do this when emailing cold prospects and trying to get an appointment, your picture will trip up their spam filter**.

- If you value your time, you won't include your phone number. Why make it so easy to call you? You aren't so desperate for their business that you will drop everything you are doing and take their call anytime they choose.

- You aren't a doctor on-call in an emergency room, you are a highly skilled sales professional who is SELECTIVE about who you work with, and you are BUSY, and <u>your process</u> requires prospects to email you first, to set up an appointment, or however you prefer.

- Remember, this effort is also about positioning yourself as a value-provider (cat), and not a chasing salesperson (dog)!

10. Get Better at Follow-up Emails After Meetings and Presentations

- After you've met with someone, and presented a solution, resist the urge to send an email with the words "following up", or "checking in".
- No two phrases have been repeated more by a salespeople to their prospects.
- I learned this from Jeremy Miner, a successful sales trainer who does a lot of social media. Look him up.
- Most follow-ups look something like this, very weak and low status:
  - *Hey Geoff, I'm just following up about our call last week, do you have any questions? We'd really like to work with you, we'd really like to partner with you. Please email me back!*
- Become more detached, act as if you don't need this sale, and you have the keys to the kingdom. Adopt the feeling that if they don't buy your product or service, it will have zero impact on you while their problems stay the same and nothing ever changes for them.
  - *Hey Jim, tried to reach you a few times, but didn't hear back ...Where do you think we should go from here?*

- This lowers their guard.
- Try to eliminate the word *follow up* and *checking in* altogether.
- Those psychologically trigger the idea that you are chasing and selling, here's a better alternative:
  - *Hey John, I know we spoke a couple of months ago about you getting higher quality leads and scaling up to $10M a month (problem/objective). Have you guys given up on that? What happened?*

Real World Examples of Good and Bad Cold Emails

Here is an email from a salesperson with a very weak approach, who I've never met before. These are the kinds of emails I used to send, and 10 years ago this type of email probably worked.

But today? I'd be surprised if this person is getting *any*

response to this email. What's wrong with it? Plenty! Here are some of the upgrades I would suggest:

- It sounds like a robot wrote this email, and it's possible they are using an artificial intelligence type of software to send mass emails. It certainly reads like it.
- First, I would confirm **WHO** this email should go to. *(I'm not our buyer for this type of product/service— another person is, information easily obtained by looking at our website.)*
- Upgrade the subject line – the headline of emails is the subject line – and when emailing people who don't know you ... **it determines if your email gets opened or not.** In this example I would suggest a specific benefit to the industry they are targeting, vs. a very generic, robot-sounding "increase your corporate revenue."
- Then, tap into the real pain of this industry – I don't see any pain mentioned.
- Why are you uniquely positioned to help?
- And provide an educational bridge to the prospect so they can learn more about your product/service in a lower-threshold way, such as a demo, a white paper, or a presentation on industry trends. This email just pointed me to their website, and when I visited, nothing was there to guide me further along my path to purchase.
- Also, I would mention other clients relevant to the target prospect—in this example, any other college they are already working with.

My Version

Subject Line:
Top 5 Trends Impacting Ticket Sales for Athletics Departments

Dear Shawn,

My name is Shane, and I help athletic departments (like Ball State) overcome stagnant ticket sales with our new proprietary mobile-location marketing platform—there is nothing like it currently in your industry. We have had success at your peer schools like Toledo and Akron. In fact, Jeff Johnson from Akron mentioned Ball State might also be a good fit.

*We recently concluded an extensive research study to help our athletics department clients, **The Top 5 Trends Impacting Ticket Sales for Division I Athletics Departments**. Would you be interested in hearing the results? I could do this in a 30-minute video call or come visit with you in person. I would love to see your new facilities. Here are some available times you can go ahead and schedule through my automated calendar by clicking this link: Calendar Link*

Can't wait to catch up with you!

Then, using my schedule send, I would create emails #2 and #3 and schedule them to be sent with about 7-10 days in between if there is no response. Those two emails are very similar to the first one, just summarizing the benefits of meeting with me. I would schedule them to be sent on

Tuesday–Thursday or even on the weekend, when fewer emails are competing for my prospect's attention.

If there is still no response, I would print out my first email and snail mail it with a sticky note on the email – *Wanted to make sure you didn't miss this!* If there is *still* no response, I would call this person about a week after my email in the mail was delivered.

Provided you are calling on a qualified prospect, one who has a good lifetime value potential – THIS is the kind of effort needed to break through today, but the effort described here is more of a marketing effort, rather than a thoughtless, lifeless cold call or cold email.

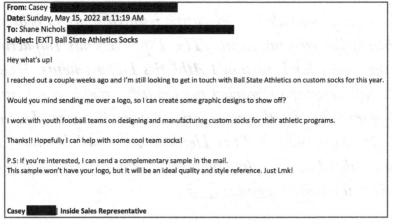

Here is a clever example of a good sales email. This is the third email I received from this rep over a 3-month period. I like that she's offering value in the form of a free design AND sample of Ball State themed socks.

[EXT] **Question**

☺ ↰ ↰ ↱

MH ○ ▓▓▓▓▓▓▓▓▓▓▓▓▓▓▓▓▓▓▓▓▓▓▓▓▓▓▓▓

Today at 8:46 AM

To: ⊗ ▓▓▓▓▓▓▓▓▓▓

Hi ▓▓▓▓

Would $220K/year revenue put a dent in your targets?

Imagine '*Cardinals Mobile*', a mobile network designed for fans to get calls, text, data and perks tied to your team. With just ~2K fans on the network you would earn ~$220K/year.

At PassionFruit we white-label mobile networks for teams and run everything in the background. We don't charge any upfront or ongoing fees.

Worth a chat?

Thanks,

▓▓▓▓▓▓

▓▓▓▓▓▓▓▓▓

CEO & Co-Founder at PassionFruit

▓▓▓▓▓▓▓▓▓

LinkedIn
www.passionfruit.fyi
Dublin, Ireland

If this isn't your jam, please let me know.

I also love this email. Short, to the point, offering value. The only thing I would change is to remove the unsubscribe, and the heart image.

Chapter Eighteen

Using Your Own Media to Advertise Your Lead Magnets

Most businesses have some form of their own media, like a website, a newsletter, social media accounts, or even a visible sign on a busy road.

I used to work in newspaper, TV and radio selling advertising to local business owners and advertising agencies. Our clients were our readers, viewers and listeners. Our best prospects were our readers, viewers and listeners.

Yet none of my former media employers ever ran any lead generation marketing using their own powerful – and free media. And that's a big miss if you ask me.

Even today, in a more challenging sales environment, you will rarely see huge media companies doing any advertising on their own media, perhaps it's because they don't know how to get results, perhaps they should read my book!

Any available media should *all* be used to market your lead magnets in addition to any paid marketing efforts.

Why? Because they are free to you! Anything you control that attracts eyeballs, regardless of who and how many, should be used to promote your lead magnets.

Overseeing sponsorship for a Division 1 NCAA athletics program has its advantages, and one of those advantages is I have several media options where I can market my lead magnets for free and reach many good prospects.

My media options include:

- **Radio commercials** in the live broadcasts of our football and basketball games. Our games are broadcast on local radio, and some are streamed on Sirius XM Radio. I run at least one radio ad during all games. Here is a simple :30 radio script I wrote, it's basically my elevator pitch:
  - Hello, I'm Shane Nichols, I'm in charge of sponsorship for Ball State Athletics. And I can help your business profit from the Ball State Community, the largest economic force in the region, a community you should target if you want to grow your business. We can do this better than any other type of advertising. I guarantee we can make it work—measurably. To learn more, take the Ball State Biz Quiz. Just visit Ball State Sports Dot Com Slash Profit, *that's Ball State Sports Dot Com Slash Profit. Go Cards!*
- **Print ads** in our official game-day programs – we distribute printed and digital versions of a basketball

and a football program at all games and through our website.

- **Display ads** on our official website reaching over a million people per year. Our website is the marketing platform I get the most exposure from, with little cost to me, so I run display ads year-round promoting my quiz and my *10 Ways to Profit* guide. When someone clicks on my ad, it leads them to a landing page where they can access both lead magnets.

- **Social media posts** on our business LinkedIn, Facebook, Twitter, and Instagram pages. Athletics controls their social feeds, so I don't do much marketing there because their accounts are for entertaining fans. But we have our own sponsorship-specific feeds, and I've made efforts to post content and gain followers. This is time consuming and hasn't worked as well as my other media options. I go into greater detail on social media in the next chapter.

- **Signage** at our sporting events. I have placed banners visible to fans who attend our football and basketball games.

- **Email signatures**. I covered this already in chapter 17. I include a link to access my guide or quiz in all of me outgoing emails. This can be especially effective when sending follow-up emails to prospects who are just getting to know you.

What If I Don't Have Any Media Available to Me?

Most businesses don't have many media options under their control beyond a corporate website and that's ok, because this gives you the opportunity to convert your website into a lead generating machine.

How?

By transforming it from a brochure of random information into a funnel type landing page that promotes your lead magnets. When someone decides to visit your website, there is a reason, so give them direction. When they arrive, steer them towards your lead magnets, capture their contact information – then follow up. Now you have a lead, instead of a ghostly visitor!

One of my sponsors, Randy Stoops of Stoops Buick GMC, is a great example. Many potential auto buyers visit his website to view his new and used inventory, but before they can access this desirable information, he requires they input their email address. Now he has a lead for his salespeople to follow up with.

Will this repel some visitors? Sure. But we're in the business of sales, and repelling unqualified traffic lets you invest more time and energy on the qualified ones. Transforming your website into a lead generation landing page may not produce a ton of leads, but it will produce more than the brochure version, I can 100% guarantee that!

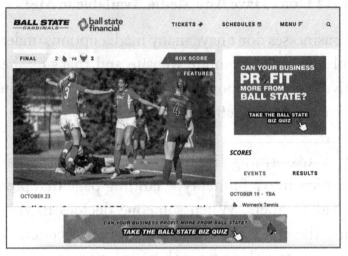

Here are examples of display ads running on our official athletics website.

This is a full-page print ad that ran in our basketball and football programs.

More display ads on our website.

*This was a social media post that ran on our
Facebook and Instagram accounts.*

*This is a banner I hang at our football and basketball
venues driving traffic to my landing page.*

Chapter Nineteen

Social Media—the Obligatory Chapter

If you've read the entire book up to this point, thank you. Here is my obligatory recognition of the greatest media of the moment – social media!

It could be my age, my generational bias, or just a hunch, but social media (to me) is just a *complement* to my other marketing efforts.

It's not THE answer, it's just another type of media – one immensely popular today.

Put me in a different market, with a different product to sell, and I might think differently. But here at Ball State, where I'm limited geographically, social media is a very small piece of my overall lead generation effort. And I've had no problem consistently hitting sales goals without using much social media.

In my experience, **direct communication** is simply a better way to build a bond with business customers, the same way it deepens relationships in your personal life.

Imagine how your family and friends would respond if you only talked to them through Facebook? Probably not well.

The direct marketing tactics I recommend represent **a local effort**, *a contrarian effort*, and most importantly, a personalized effort – and that's why they continue to work for sales professionals like me.

Can you reach business owners on social media? Absolutely. Many sellers already use social media, and maybe you do too. In my business we commonly announce new sponsors via social media. But giving *shout-outs* to clients is more of a retention tactic, and it's a smart thing to do, but it's not technically generating any leads.

Prioritize Your Time and Strengths

I only have so much time in the day, and I don't have a huge budget, so I'm choosy about where I spend my time and where I advertise for leads. And I don't have an interest in or strength for posting anything on social media. I never have. Perhaps you do. If so, don't let me discourage you, but social media is not a strength of mine.

While I have personal accounts on most of the major social media platforms, I don't want to use my personal feeds to solicit anybody. The only exception would be LinkedIn, where I plan on promoting this book, because the content will be relevant and helpful to many of my connections.

But in my sponsorship business, I'm selling to business owners in a specific geographical area, not my high school and college pals on Facebook, nor my colleagues and former co-workers on LinkedIn.

Could some of my friends and social connections be good prospects for sponsorship? Maybe, but a proven way to repel any new prospect is by acting like the typical eager salesperson trying to sell something to all their friends and family. This is commonly done in life insurance or real estate sales and is part of the reason so many people fail in those jobs.

Realize this: *You can live without social media.* Extinguish all fears of missing out on the latest social media craze, because there are plenty of other (proven) ways to generate leads and land appointments without ever having to solicit your friends or family!

Realize You Have Zero Ownership of Your Followers

All your followers, and people who like your posts, even the people who directly message you on social media – please understand *you have zero ownership of this list or group* unless you can obtain their email address and offline contact information. If your prospect list lives within the social media platform, you do not have a database – <u>the social media company does.</u>

And in an instant, they can change their rules on privacy and advertising, and *you could lose all your followers, even have your entire account suspended, and there is nothing you can do about it.*

In fact, this happens regularly. As I am finalizing this chapter, Apple has made it more difficult for apps like Facebook and Twitter to use your data to sell advertising. Apple can do this because they own the distribution channel – your smart phone. Facebook recently changed their algorithm and now it favors content from friends and families over commercial messages.

If you take away nothing else from this book, please realize how important it is to have your own accurate personal list of existing clients, past clients, and warm prospects.

And on that list, you have their physical mailing address, email address, work phone number, cell phone number, and even their home address in some cases. This list is one of your most valuable assets as a B2B seller.

The Most Competitive Shark-Infested Pool of Marketers on Earth

Most social media advertising is consumer based (B2C – businesses selling to consumers), except for LinkedIn. And because platforms like Facebook, Twitter, and Instagram have millions of users, they attract the most aggressive, successful, experienced marketers on earth. Those marketers may or may not be competitors of your product or service – but … they can *steal attention away from you* AND outspend you, outlast you, and share more content and build better lead magnets than you, making your efforts to get noticed feel like sending smoke signals on a windy day.

Here's the thing: *when you dive into the treacherous sea of social media, you will encounter more competition than any other type of media in the world.* You will be competing against the largest, most advanced e-commerce (and even now, brick and mortar businesses), plus an ocean's worth of other marketers.

I recently read that over 350 million photos are uploaded to Facebook *each day*. And that 720,000 hours of video are uploaded to YouTube *each day*. And on average, over 500 million tweets are shared *each day*.

To me, it seems like everyone is in the social media pool, and the smart thing to do is **get out**.

Buying Advertising Successfully on Social Media Requires Expertise You Don't Have

I used to buy traditional media for large grocery chains like Albertsons and Safeway – and you know why they paid me to buy their media? Partly to get fair and below-market pricing. As a former seller, I knew the fair market values for local television, newspaper, and radio airtime.

But also, they were paying me to outsource a mundane, confusing, and time-consuming activity, the act of *media buying*. A good salesperson should often outsource this activity to a qualified professional or risk wasting a lot of money.

Even buying traditional media like television and radio is confusing to the layperson. Each has its own language, full of jargon specific to that industry. Ever heard of a GRP, CPP, or CPM?

The same barriers exist in social media – it's so confusing there is now an entire industry of experts and specialists for every type of social media.

When you venture beyond posting on your personal or

business page, when you enter the arena of buying advertising on social media, *you are entering a very effective digital vacuum that can empty your bank account FAST!* And even worse, there's usually no sales rep to help you. Unless you are spending millions of dollars, the best you can hope for is an online chat with a customer service team often based in India.

If you plan on spending money advertising on any social media platform, I strongly urge you to hire an experienced buyer – while bearing in mind that the results from your advertising are just mostly dependent on your *bait*. Even the best media buyer on earth can't get results with bad bait.

The World's Largest and Most Visible Public Complaint Box

In essence, for most local businesses, social media has become one giant *public* complaint box – the exact opposite of the original purpose of the complaint box, whose complaints could only be seen by management, *because they were locked in a box!!*

Today, a vocal minority, even non-customers, can *derail all your social media efforts* with negative comments, feedback, and ratings.

One of our sponsors, Greg Hubler, the owner of the local Ford and Hyundai dealership in Muncie, just opened a beautiful new campus featuring both dealerships. They spent millions of dollars; the project took years to fund, plan, and finally construct. The design reflects the Ford Motor company's entire history of experience and research into what customers want in a retail auto shopping experience. Yet here is a recent review from a customer on a social media review site, giving Hubler 1 out of 5 stars:

> *Pleasant employees. Quick Service. The new facility is pretty awful. Ugly, cold, and gray punctuated with small "pops" of orange that some decorator must have told them was cool. The "quiet room" furniture was not comfortable, and the room was far from quiet. Loud country-sounding music seeping in and making it hard to read my book. Another customer agreed with me. So glad my recall didn't take too long. I still love Fords.*

My advice here: Get used to **not** pleasing everyone. Customers can get good, reasonable, and even superior service and *still find reasons to complain online.* For some, this is all they do each day! And this means you need to spend more time responding to and resolving all complaints immediately, before they spiral into something worse – like going viral.

What's Popular Today May Vanish in an Instant

Doesn't it feel like social media has been a thing for a long time now?

Seems like ages. The reality is many social media platforms eventually fail. And the services that are wildly popular today haven't been in business that long. It reminds me of the fickle fashion industry. What's in style today can be out of style next week.

Facebook has been around for less than two decades. YouTube, Instagram, Snapchat, Twitter? All about 20 years old. TikTok just got started in 2016.

Here is a list of formerly popular failures in social media:

- Google Wave and Google Buzz
- Friendster
- Google Plus
- Vine
- Myspace
- iTunes Ping
- Meerkat

My point? Nothing in the social media world is guaranteed to be popular forever.

But the United States Postal Service (USPS) has been delivering mail since 1792. FedEx started delivering express packages back in 1973.

What Other Successful Sellers Do on Social Media

Now, if you still want to spend time on social media, please take some advice from one of the savviest social media marketers on earth – Russell Brunson, co-founder of the business software company Click Funnels.

In his book, *Traffic Secrets*, he outlines the social media strategy that helped him, and his team, build one of the most successful software companies in the world. And it's a strategy adopted now by thousands of young entrepreneurs building their own businesses.

I strongly urge you to read all three of his books. Start with *Dotcom Secrets*, then read *Expert Secrets*, then read *Traffic Secrets* last – this is a trilogy of books best read in order.

Treat Social Media Like a Party

First and foremost, Brunson made the decision to be a social media producer instead of a *social media consumer*, meaning his sole purpose was to grow his business, rather than scroll through cat videos all day. He suggests *focusing your profile on business* and to start producing content that will engage and attract your ideal clients. If you must, keep a personal profile; use it for personal stuff, and create a business profile for marketing.

Here is another very general, high-level summary of what the best marketers do on social media: the most successful ones **don't try to hard-sell you anything when they post content.** Early on in his social marketing efforts, Brunson spent much of his time trying to *sell* on Facebook, Twitter, and Instagram, with very little success.

Then he noticed one of his mentors, internet marketer Perry Belcher, never posted anything with a hard sell. Instead, he treated social media like a party: engaging with guests, showing interest in others, introducing people who might help each other, offering advice, but never selling anything. And it was working, because Belcher converted many of his new friends into paying customers, *but only after they got to know each other.*

Think about it, how much time would you spend with

someone at a party who is not only a stranger, but constantly trying to sell you something? Very little.

Consumers spend time on social media because they seek the stimulation of interacting with others; they want to build relationships; they want to learn about news, trends, and the opinions of others. They want to watch funny videos about cats and dogs.

You can sell them something after they become curious enough about you to visit your home page or profile.

Your home page is where people learn what you do – where you can display offers and provide educational bridges for visitors to learn about your products and services. Then, ideally, you can capture their contact information and move them into your own database.

Here are a few things to focus on if you dive further into B2B social media marketing:

1. **Focus first on the social media platform most of your customers are on:**
   You should **focus on just one social media platform first,** because being effective will take *regular effort.* In B2B sales, your best choice is LinkedIn. It's worth investing in the Sales Navigator, which gives you upgraded search tools and the ability to send direct messages even if you aren't connected to a prospect. You also get better insights on who is interacting with the content you post. You can post here, or you can utilize it for sending direct messaging which is what I prefer.

2. **Decide where you are posting from:**

I also recommend you create a business profile and use that as your base instead of your personal profile. I rarely post anything on my personal LinkedIn feed because my feed isn't targeted for my sponsorship sales business. Same with Facebook. My personal feed reaches my friends, family, and co-workers. But I do have a sponsorship business page, and this is where I focus my marketing on LinkedIn. This is a personal choice of mine; you may feel differently and do this all from your own personal page. It's ultimately your choice.

3. **Optimize your profile:**

When prospects visit your LinkedIn profile (and/or business page), it should be immediately clear what you can do for them, starting with your headline. Your headline should be some shorter summary of your elevator speech. Before you do any profile optimization, check out the great book by LinkedIn marketing expert Adam Houlahan, *The LinkedIn Playbook*. It is the most updated advice on how to optimize a LinkedIn profile. Hint: copy what he does, and you'll be on your way!

4. **Follow, connect, and engage with the people you are targeting:**

In his book *The LinkedIn Playbook*, Houlahan describes the strategy he uses as a business owner to connect with and engage his dream targets. First, he advises that you develop five pre-written scripts for interacting with new connections. There is the *connection-request message*, a *welcome message* for new connections, and a *congratulations message* for anniversaries, work milestones, birthdays, etc. Then there is a *gift message* for sharing an educational resource (lead magnet) rather than asking for an appointment or sale. The final script is a *keep in touch* message where you periodically share some insight, value, or an article you feel would be of interest to your prospect. The idea here is, each message is personalized, and shows you care and put actual thought into reaching out.

5. **Organically grow your audience by engaging and posting valuable content:**
This goes back to positioning. If you want to be a thought leader and create your own content, do that. Or you can be one who curates and shares relevant news with your followers and associates. The type and volume of content you post will vary based on which social platform you are using, but realize that even on LinkedIn, you should be posting something at least once per day.

6. **Then consider buying ads for faster growth:**
Advertising options vary on each platform. Facebook has the most robust targeting and advertising options, but it's also the most confusing to figure out. On LinkedIn there are advertising options I won't bore you with here. Again, I recommend you work with a specialized buyer for each platform.

In future editions of this book, perhaps my views will change about social media.

But in the next chapter, I'm going to introduce you to a powerful marketing campaign that has proven to *double, triple, even quadruple sales* for those who embrace it. And, you don't have to use *any social media* for it to work.

Interested?

Shane

Francis Bacon said Knowledge is Power.

I can show you how you can hold the power too.
We can inundate your business with leads that you can convert to sales.
Technology plus massive resources will really turn your head.

Intrigued – please connect.

Revenue Development Specialist

View profile   Accept

I thought this was a clever way to send a connection request. At the very least, whenever you ask to connect with someone you don't personally know, give them a reason.

Here is a great example of using an educational bridge to attract prospects. Notice Tony Robbins isn't trying to sell anybody anything, that comes later.

Chapter Twenty

The Persistent Salesperson's Way to Riches

Ok, by now, I've shared a lot of different ideas with you. And yes, they all require a little more planning than just picking up the phone and calling a prospect cold. Or, sending them an email out of the blue.

This is true, **it is more work,** but achieving high-level selling success in a competitive marketplace (when nobody is giving you leads) simply requires a different approach today.

But this effort is totally worth it, because you will make more money, hit your sales goals, gain the respect and trust of your employer and fellow salespeople, and retire from the drudgery of cold calling!

To put it simply, making this extra effort will **empower** you.

And as an employee, being left alone to do your own

thing – because they all know you're good at your job – is about as good as it gets when you work for someone else.

But I also realize, because I am also under the same daily pressure, that you (as a salesperson) *need to move the needle* – and fast.

So, here is a marketing campaign that combines some old-school sales hustle with clever marketing and **should become your cornerstone strategy for developing new business**.

The Dream 100

Many of the most successful marketing gurus you hear about today started with some form of the strategy I'm about to describe here.

I've mentioned marketing expert Russell Brunson a few times already; he and his Click Funnels team built their entire software business on the heels of this very strategy. It works so well, they've never had to raise venture capital, which is unusual for software start-ups.

It starts with identifying your very best possible buyers, or what Chet Holmes, author of the best-selling book *The Ultimate Sales Machine*, describes as your **Dream 100**.

Don't get too caught up on the number, just grasp the idea of getting the attention of just your dream prospects. I'm talking about the people *you are certain spend the most money on the same type of product or service you sell*.

Holmes became famous for his ability to double sales almost everywhere he went. His most celebrated success came early in his career, working for Charles Munger, the late Vice Chairman of Berkshire Hathaway, and business partner to Warren Buffett. Munger was the other guy sitting onstage next to Buffett during their famous investor summits in Omaha, Nebraska.

Munger put Holmes in charge of a magazine that was ranked last in advertising revenue in its category. They had a database of 2200 advertisers who Holmes and team regularly cold-called with little success.

Then one day, after doing some research, Holmes realized just 167 of those 2200 advertisers bought 95% of all advertising in their competitors' magazines.

That's about 8% of the market buying 95% of all advertising.

You may be familiar with a concept called Pareto's Principle, more commonly known as the 80/20 rule. While the percentages are different here, the principle is the same: *A very small number of inputs are responsible for most outputs.*

Holmes and team abandoned all other prospects and went full-bore on these 167 best possible buyers. They created a long-term marketing campaign that involved sending sales letters every two weeks along with follow-up calls.

But they didn't just send letters – they sent gifts too, ensuring their direct effort stood out even more. They sent fun gifts like Rubik's Cubes, pen flashlights, magnifying glasses, mini calculators. Stuff that can be sourced cheaply, but also something a prospect might fancy and keep on their desk.

With this marketing effort, his team eventually landed 30 of those 167 best potential buyers. But they didn't get a single response *until the 4ᵗʰ month of this campaign.* That's 12 weeks of mailing letters, and fun gifts, and making regular follow-up calls.

This effort takes prospective clients on a journey like this:

1. I've never heard of your company.
2. What is this company I keep hearing about?
3. I think I've heard of this company.
4. Yes, I've heard of this company.
5. Yes, I do business with this company.

AND, because these were their dream buyers, each of the 30 clients spent **big**. They bought full-page ads, two-page spreads, premium positions, and inked long-term commitments. Once you gain the trust of a dream buyer, your effort will be rewarded because they buy a lot, and they pay their bills!

Those 30 advertisers alone were enough to double sales from the previous year. In fact, over the next three years, Holmes doubled their sales **each year** and landed most of the 167 on their dream list.

This strategy relies on the fact that prospects will eventually recognize and reward your persistence in the face of their resistance. But success requires a dash of creativity, like good sales letters, fun gifts, and providing a compelling reason to meet with you.

Offer to <u>Educate</u> Your Prospects on Industry Trends

Holmes is a big believer in *selling by educating*. So, your hook or offer can't be <u>just asking for an appointment to sell them something</u>. Rather, you should offer to **educate them** about trends in their industry, like an executive briefing about *The 5 Most Dangerous Trends Facing… (whatever their industry)*. Educate first, position yourself as a provider of value, get the appointment, sell later.

Sound familiar? It's just a mini-lead magnet. Time and time again, as I discover and learn about the most effective marketing techniques from countless books and courses, **some form of educating is always involved**. In this case, keep it simple; look to compile an executive briefing, a white paper, or presentation on something trending in their industry.

Before I created my *10 Ways to Profit* lead magnet, I advertised a research report authored by a distinguished professor at Ball State University as my *educational* lead magnet.

This report offered compelling evidence that any business owner was missing out on a huge opportunity by not catering to the Ball State Community, and because it wasn't marketed well by the university, it seemed none of my prospects had ever heard about it.

You can create, borrow, buy, or compile something just as compelling for your own prospects.

The Power of Focus

In this campaign, you will deliberately put all your focus on just the best buyers in your industry and *ignore all other prospects*. **The only leads you're concerned with now are those who are the very top spenders on your product or service. Period.**

And it may take some market research to determine who these people are. You need the identify the decision maker, or decision makers, and along with their names you need their phone number, mailing address, email address, and connect with them on LinkedIn.

Another advantage to this strategy is using every follow-up as an opportunity to collect valuable data from these dream buyers. Every follow-up should result in discovering some bit of information – like getting the email address of your prospect if you don't already have it.

Or, confirming who else is involved in the decision-making process. You can collect this type of data from gatekeepers who protect your decision makers. Good salespeople do this instinctively – like you – should do this instinctively on every outreach.

The letters and gifts are designed to elevate awareness for your follow-up calls. The follow-up calls are for nothing more than setting up an appointment, or to collect more information that will help on the next follow-up. Simple as that.

Cruise Control

Are you one of those people who drives long distances on the interstate and never uses your cruise control? Are you that person I pass six or seven different times because you're just aimlessly driving along at varying rates of speed? I do not understand you and your random acts of driving. Cruise control is a wonderful invention that lets you sit back and focus on the task at hand … driving.

That's why this campaign works best when you create a calendar detailing every action you will take for at least 6 months. There is a cadence for when letters are mailed, when they are to arrive, and when you will follow up with a phone call.

There should be at least a few touches per month. And the letters should be accompanied by creative little gifts, which should be selected and sourced ahead of time. Instead of random acts of cold calling and cold emailing, you follow the calendar, and your campaign will run smoothly and efficiently … like it's on cruise control.

Investing in Marketing Becomes Your Competitive Advantage

By now, I hope you recognize your biggest advantage as a B2B seller – you sell something that has a high average sale, and/or a high lifetime customer value. This allows you to profitably invest in marketing campaigns (like this one) to get the attention of your dream prospects.

It becomes your advantage because most of your

competitors won't do it. But here YOU are … investing in gifts, postage, time, and effort. While your competitors are asleep at the wheel, you're stealthily winning the hearts and minds of your potential dream buyers.

Knowing all along that you need only one sale to make this effort worth it. But if you truly commit to this type of campaign, you will land more than one of your dream clients, or you're doing something wrong!

Don't Stop—Ever

Holmes says in his book:

> *"By being pigheaded, persistent, and determined and by continually finding more clever and aggressive ways to get in front of these dream buyers, you actually earn their respect in the long haul."*

It took Holmes four straight months of zero results until he got one dream buyer. But once one of *your* dream buyers comes on board, your prospects will notice (because you will tell them in your next letter and follow-up phone call), and then it becomes a tidal wave of success.

Here is a summary of steps to get you started:

1. **Compile a list of dream clients.** You should know each one's name, title, phone number, and mailing address. *There should be no doubt about the ability of these people to spend money on your exact product or service.* This will determine the size of your list. If

you only find 40 perfect prospects, no problem. If you find over 100, consider how much you want to invest, because there are expenses here. It's fine to stop at 100, even if you leave a few out. You can always go back to them later. LinkedIn and their company website should have enough info to get you started. The research tool Data Axle available from the library that I spoke about in Chapter 16 is another way to obtain this information.

2. **Create a calendar** and pinpoint your outreach efforts.

3. **Decide on trinkets/toys/other things** you're going to send in the mail and purchase them ahead of time.

4. **Find something educational to offer** to your prospective clients that they will find valuable. Realize they are stuck in their day-to-day routines, and don't have time or the perspective you do as an objective outsider, someone who can do some research and report on the most important trends impacting their industry. It's often worth it to hire someone to find or compile this for you – a researcher, writer, there are plenty of freelance resources.

5. **Now, write a one-page (two-sided) sales letter.** This does not have to be complicated. Here, step-by-step, is all you have to write:

   a. Dear Client,

   b. I'm so and so (your elevator pitch).

   c. As a gesture of goodwill, we've compiled a 30-minute high-level, executive briefing about the top 5 trends impacting your industry...

   d. That's why I included a Rubik's Cube with this letter, because you never know what combination of information will take your business to the next level...

   e. These are the other clients who have enjoyed our presentation....

   f. I think you'll find it helpful, relevant, insightful... here are some dates to choose from...

   g. I will follow up on xx date to schedule a time...

   h. To your success, (your name, title, etc.).

   i. P.S. Include a testimonial or two from existing clients. If you don't have any testimonials, reach out to your five best clients, write something for them, and ask them to approve it.

6. **Send the letter** using tactics I described in Chapter 16.

7. **Use the same letter** for future mailings if necessary; just be sure to change the date! Even better, incorporate the sequencing techniques covered earlier.

I estimate if you follow these steps and never quit, and keep getting more and more creative with your efforts, you should convert around 10% (or more) of your Dream 100 into clients – each year. Those 10 new clients should be worth more than six, possibly seven figures in lifetime sales value.

How much will you spend? Depends on the size of your list and what kind of gifts you offer but this effort will be extremely profitable for most B2B products and services.

Chapter Twenty-One

My Results Generating Leads at Ball State Athletics from 2021 – 2025

What I've covered in the previous chapters are essentially two strategies working together to replace random, cold outreach to find new clients:

1. **Active Outbound** marketing campaigns designed to get the attention of, and appointments with – high quality cold prospects – using various media including direct mail, email marketing, LinkedIn, chamber marketing etc.

2. A **Passive Automated Inbound** marketing campaign *always* running in the background, on any available free media, sending traffic to a vanity URL (ballStatesports.com/profit), where prospects are sent to a funnel type landing page, able to engage with educational resources, appealing to prospects in

any stage of their buying process, capturing contact information in exchange those resources.

What I can say, with absolute certainty, from my own experience, from what I've observed from the most successful sales organizations, having an outbound and inbound lead generation marketing strategy – even a bad one – generates more leads than NOT having one.

Before I detail my results, and before you make any judgements about your ability to apply these two strategies to your own situation, I'd like to highlight some of the challenges I face selling sponsorships for Ball State Athletics.

Ball State University is based in Muncie, Indiana, an hour northeast of Indianapolis just off I-69, residing in the second poorest county in the state, still recovering from a staggering loss of factory jobs in the 1990's.

Almost every large company once headquartered here has closed, moved, or been acquired by a larger out-of-state company. Muncie is now a town of franchises, regional offices, and distribution centers. We have fans, but not many attend our sporting events. Most of our alumni (about 200,000 of them – I am also an alum) live within two hours of campus, yet very few will ever attend a sporting event after they graduate. Many don't attend sporting events while they are here in school!

We struggle to fill even a quarter of our venues with ticket-buying fans. Only when more popular teams visit, like Butler, Notre Dame, or Purdue, do we sniff a sellout.

The one thing that could generate interest among our disenchanted alumni is **winning** – specifically in Indiana, *winning in basketball.* But sadly, neither of our basketball teams have made the NCAA tournament in 25 years.

It doesn't help that nearby Indianapolis is one of the most dynamic sports cities in the country boasting franchises from the NFL, NBA, WNBA, and collegiate programs like IU, Purdue, Butler (Notre Dame also nearby), and minor league baseball, hockey, basketball, soccer, and soon – volleyball. All sucking interest and sponsorship dollars away from our program.

2021-22 Season

I began implementing these two strategies right after pandemic. Because fans weren't allowed to attend games that year I lost over half of our sponsorship revenue, about $500,000.

The following year, the 2021-22 season, I was determined to hit my sales goals without cold prospecting. I ran weekly ads with 3 different chambers of commerce. I mailed sales letters to my list of prospects. I ran radio ads during our games, carpeted our website with display ads, and even tried some paid LinkedIn and Facebook advertising.

I made zero cold telephone calls and sent zero cold emails to prospects <u>the entire year</u>.

This was very risky for someone in my position – being solely responsible for a six-figure revenue goal while the economy rebounded from a world-wide pandemic. And believe me, I did not share my strategy with my employer! But for the entire selling season, instead of cold prospecting, I simply advertised my lead magnets and followed up with leads who responded.

And as a result, for the 20-21 season:

- I *attracted* 6 new clients from my marketing – they reached out to me. More responded but I didn't close them all.
- Made up all lost revenue from the previous year – about $500k.
- Crushed my sales goal.
- Maximized my bonus.
- I was recognized by my employer with an award for **Property of the Year** for selling excellence amongst my peers.

You might be thinking, only 6 new clients Shane? Yes. I only closed 6 new accounts. That's not a ton. But *dozens more raised their hand*, <u>invited me into their world for future follow-up</u>, and many became sponsors the following season.

My educational marketing tools (lead magnets) warmed them up to where they would listen, trust, and meet with me in the future. Plus, prospects who responded to my marketing were easier to close – typically done in one meeting – and a few I closed over the phone. I noticed prospects who absorbed our educational resources were more *primed to buy*, and they treated me different, not as a salesperson, but as a *value provider*.

However, the true benefit wasn't the new business

landed – effortlessly – it was the **time and focus I was able to spend on warm prospects and existing clients.** <u>This</u> is why I hit my sales goals and made up all the lost revenue from the pandemic.

2022-23 Season

During the 2022-23 season, two of my largest sponsors were both acquired by larger companies headquartered outside of Muncie – and the new ownership promptly cut their local marketing and laid off staff. These two clients were 15% of my gross revenue – or about $135,000. Coming off my award-winning 2021-22 season, I doubted my lead generation strategy could plug this gap. On top of losing the two accounts, my sales goal was increased to pre-pandemic levels; I now had to find over $300,000 of new revenue to achieve my sales goal, in Muncie.

But I soldiered on and kept on marketing, *and once again I made zero cold calls and sent zero cold emails to any prospects during the entire selling season.* I refreshed my advertising with new creative and tweaked my lead magnets. In the spring of 2022, the peak selling time for the upcoming football season, I began my Dream 100 direct mail campaign.

I was prepared to send 6 sales letters leading up to first kick. Each letter included some lumpy item or gift, with hooks, stories, rationale, an offer, and a deadline. By the time I got to letter #5 in early August, I had *attracted* 15 new clients. By the end of October, I was up to **25 new sponsors** who responded to my campaign. I ended up hitting my sales goal by the end of October. I also won another award; my employer named me **General Manager of the Year** among my peer group for selling excellence.

2023-24, 2024-25 Seasons

I will summarize the past two selling seasons as follows:

- My lead generation efforts produce about 20 – 30 solid leads each year. Our response has gone down as we have saturated the market. But as new businesses open, new opportunities arise, and new prospects are exposed to our strategy, we continue to develop leads.
- We generate WAY MORE leads than before I implemented the two strategies. I remember maybe getting 2 or 3 inquiries per season when I first started.
- Most of our growth comes from renewing and upselling our existing sponsors.
- We only seem to lose clients due to corporate acquisitions, or changes in leadership. In general, because we spend more time making our clients happy, and fulfilling on their sponsorship, our sponsors stay longer.
- I rarely send any cold emails or ever make a cold call unless there is a very compelling sales angle making it worth my time.
- I maximize my compensation because I have hit my goals.
- I don't feel burned out, I'm confident in reaching our revenue goals each season, and I don't stress about finding new business.

- I trust my marketing, but I'm always tweaking and improving, spending time on innovating client-attracting marketing ideas vs. cold outreach.
- The favorite part of my job now, what gets me the most excited, is seeing my lead generation marketing work.

Results of The Ball State Biz Quiz

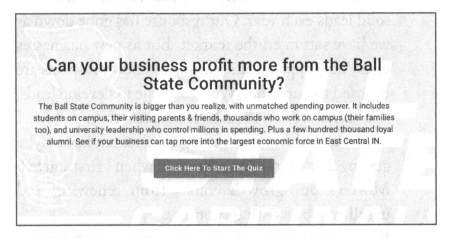

The quiz has been the most popular of my lead magnets. Quizzes arouse curiosity, they present a challenge and opportunity to learn, and despite hating them during my school days – as a lead magnet – they work great!

As of December 2024, there have been 3200 views of my quiz, with 91 leads produced. Here's the interesting part, while 3200 people have *viewed* the quiz, the completion rate is only about 57%. Why would so many people view the quiz, but not finish it?

Many aren't qualified prospects, and that's ok; this saves me time and energy from dealing with unqualified people. Also, I'm always learning and improving and tweaking the quiz so that it's helpful, informative, and easy.

And, when you ask for personal information – like an email address – sometimes it turns people off. In marketing, nothing is perfect. But I am very pleased because those who do complete the quiz are usually good prospects for m*e*. The majority have been owners and decision makers.

Downloads of My *How to Profit* Guide

As of December 2024, over 1,000 people have viewed or downloaded my *How to Profit* guide lead magnet. While the guide may not be as popular as the quiz, it's elevated my positioning among the business community, adding a layer of credibility and authority to my efforts.

Over time, as my marketing keeps running, new people discover and download the guide. If it's always available, and continually marketed, it serves as a vital educational bridge to learn more about sponsorship, all without taking any of my time.

Our best leads consume both lead magnets.

The Secrets to Sustained Selling Success

During my first two seasons at Ball State (2018-19, 2019-20) I bounced around from prospect to prospect with no real strategy. Sure, I made myself *feel and look busy*, and my employer encouraged this activity, but the net results were never reliable. And even worse, this type of cold *manic* prospecting **stole time, energy and focus away from warm prospects and existing clients with growth opportunities.**

This unsystematic approach is common in many companies. I'm sure you've heard the phrase "make more calls" rather than being offered an idea or solution that could free up your peak performance. Here's what I've concluded, making more calls and trying harder *doesn't* move the needle like it used to. **What it does do – reliably – is burn good salespeople out.**

Today, because of my inbound and outbound strategy, the prospects I know have the most potential – *those already willing and ready to hear my ideas* – get more of my energy and focus than ever before.

Here are my areas of selling priority now: **Existing happy clients who can refer others to me:** Once a year I send my existing clients a personal thank you letter, along with an incentive to refer someone to me. Referrals must be earned and asked for; don't expect them to materialize without any effort on your part. If I can't get a referral, I ask for a testimonial instead.

1. **Clients with sponsorships expiring:** In sponsorship sales, these are called renewals, and they get my full attention. Upselling existing customers is the most profitable activity you can do.

2. **Warm targets, people who are willing to meet with me and hear my ideas:** They get my full attention after my renewal clients, this sometimes includes past clients who didn't renew for a variety of reasons. This group also includes anyone who opted in for one of my lead magnets but did not buy for whatever reason.

3. **50 – 100 cold but high-value targets, people who fit the description of a perfect client for a variety of reasons:** It's easy to get sidetracked on where you should spend your valuable energy, time, and marketing funds. And others (including your boss) may have strong opinions about who your best prospects are. Here's what I have learned, narrow it down to *only those who are spending money on exactly the type of thing you already sell.* **These people have demonstrated a need,** <u>have money to satisfy the need</u>, **you can fulfill that need,** *these are the only people who qualify as dream prospects.*

It's common in my role to consider large vendors of the university as good prospects. For example, Ball State spends millions constructing massive brick buildings around campus. Any given moment there are a dozen of construction projects in various stages of completion. So, it's easy to think those construction firms might reciprocate by sponsoring our athletics program. But mostly they don't. There are very few construction firms who are big sponsors of athletics. You also won't find many construction firms doing much – if any – local marketing. Contrast this with a local car dealership, who is actively marketing in the local community. They buy a lot of advertising, they have co-op funds from their manufacturer, they sponsor all kinds of things. Is it easy to get the attention of the local car dealer? No, *but that's why you chose to invest in marketing, to get their attention and an appointment, and once you're in, expect an easier path to a sale* **because they already spend money on exactly what YOU SELL!**

Marketing Summary – What Works

After studying and practicing the past few years, here are the main things I learned that help elicit a response to my B2B marketing efforts:

1. **Spend time developing a good elevator pitch** that clearly defines the value or solution you are providing *and why you are unique*. I continue to develop mine,

and it's based on my ability to reach the Ball State Community (the most affluent group of people who live in Muncie) better than any other type of local media.

2. **Find out what key problems your prospects are having** that your products or services could resolve. Interview them; take them out for a drink. <u>This feedback is invaluable</u>. I learned my prospects doubted their ability to get measurable results from sports sponsorship. And they didn't understand the importance—or potential—of catering to the Ball State Community.

3. **Create a lead magnet**—such as a report, a guide, a quiz. Hire someone to do this if necessary. You can even license this type of content from someone else or compile it from free and publicly available information. Invest time and energy in developing the right bait. You will be rewarded for extra effort here because if it's good it can be used for a very long time.

4. **Build a landing page**. This is where you send all prospects who opt-in for your lead magnet, and ideally, their contact information is automatically captured in some type of database like a CRM or simple excel spreadsheet. This database of prospects will become your best source of future new business. AND *because they opted in*, and if they did so via your email marketing software, you now have permission to continue emailing them until they opt-out.

5. **If available, start marketing through your local Chamber of Commerce**. Attend their networking events, send email blasts with relevant offers, send sales letters to their mailing list, sponsor their events, and create offers specifically for their membership. Also look at marketing to other networking groups like the Rotary, Business Network International (BNI), Junto (https://junto.global), and more. Now that you have embraced the power of educating first, networking will be easier than ever.

6. **Never stop.** I cannot emphasize how important it is that your marketing runs systematically all the time. *You will know you are doing something right when somebody complains about seeing your ads too often.* Whenever this happens, I'm flattered. This is the power of direct marketing – you will never have someone complain about you emailing them, because they can so easily delete or block you.

7. **One to Many vs. One on One**. Speak publicly to groups of business owners and decision makers wherever they may gather. This could be at a networking event, a club like the Rotary, heck, <u>create your own events and invite your perfect prospects</u>. This is the next level of selling, where you are maximizing your time and effort by selling one-to-many vs. selling one-on-one. AND – **nothing elevates your credibility and positioning better than public speaking**. (New to public speaking or want to polish your skills? Consider Toastmasters International. Their Pathways learning experience

lets members tailor their public speaking education to their specific needs.)

8. **Keep trying new offers, new copy, new angles, and new marketing approaches**. Instead of cold calling, now I spend my time thinking of ways to attract clients through hooks, selling angles, and new offers. While writing this chapter I came up with an idea to include a paid membership to my local Chamber of Commerce as part of my sponsorship package. No other local advertising option offers this benefit. *And more importantly, this incentivizes the chamber to help me market this offer.* I love to read business magazines, obscure trade publications, and books on sales and marketing, and adapt the best ideas to my own situation.

Examples of Actual Responses

Over the next few pages, I've included some of the responses to our marketing efforts. These are not all the leads we've produced; several have called me directly when they were ready to engage.

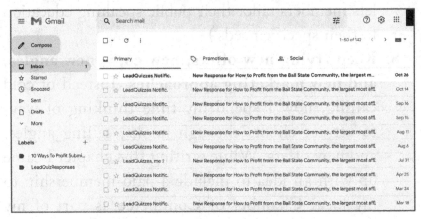

When someone takes the quiz, I get this
notification sent to my email.

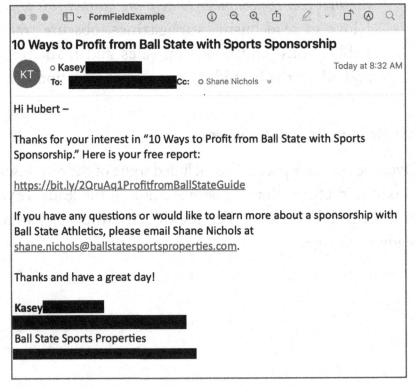

Here is a script to fulfill requests for the 10 Ways to
Profit Guide. I purposely had our coordinator fulfill
the request instead of me for positioning purposes.

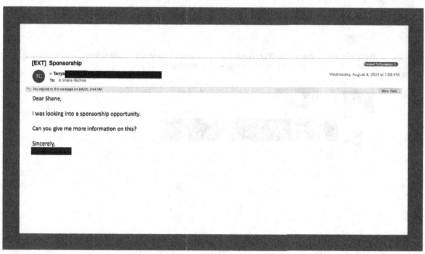

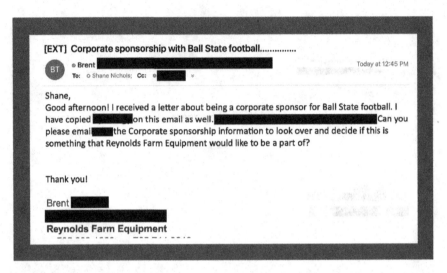

[EXT] Corporate sponsorship with Ball State football..............

BT   ● Brent ███████████████   Today at 12:45 PM
To: ○ Shane Nichols;   Cc: ● ███████ ⌄

Shane,
Good afternoon! I received a letter about being a corporate sponsor for Ball State football. I have copied ██████████ on this email as well. ████████████████████████████████ Can you please email ████ the Corporate sponsorship information to look over and decide if this is something that Reynolds Farm Equipment would like to be a part of?

Thank you!

Brent ████████
████████████████

Reynolds Farm Equipment

Hi Shane!

We received your letter in our office regarding advertising with BSU sports. I'd like to learn a bit more about what you all have to offer so let me know the next steps. Thank you!

Tyler ████████████

████████████████████████████████ Muncie, IN 47304

MARTIN

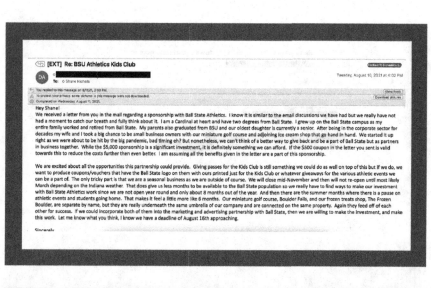

[EXT] Re: BSU Athletics Kids Club

DA   o ▮▮▮▮▮▮▮▮   Tuesday, August 10, 2021 at 4:02 PM
To: o Shane Nichols

You replied to this message on 8/11/21, 2:00 PM.
To protect your privacy, some pictures in this message were not downloaded.
Completed on Wednesday, August 11, 2021.

Hey Shane!

We received a letter from you in the mail regarding a sponsorship with Ball State Athletics. I know it is similar to the email discussions we have had but we really have not had a moment to catch our breath and fully think about it. I am a Cardinal at heart and have two degrees from Ball State. I grew up on the Ball State campus as my entire family worked and retired from Ball State. My parents also graduated from BSU and our oldest daughter is currently a senior. After being in the corporate sector for decades my wife and I took a big chance to be small business owners with our miniature golf course and adjoining ice cream shop that go hand in hand. We started it up right as we were about to be hit by the big pandemic, bad timing eh? But nonetheless, we can't think of a better way to give back and be a part of Ball State but as partners in business together. While the $5,000 sponsorship is a significant investment, it is definitely something we can afford. If the $500 coupon in the letter you sent is valid towards this to reduce the costs further then even better. I am assuming all the benefits given in the letter are a part of this sponsorship.

We are excited about all the opportunities this partnership could provide. Giving passes for the Kids Club is still something we could do as well on top of this but if we do, we want to produce coupons/vouchers that have the Ball State logo on them with ours printed just for the Kids Club or whatever giveaways for the various athletic events we can be a part of. The only tricky part is that we are a seasonal business as we are outside of course. We will close mid-November and then will not re-open until most likely March depending on the Indiana weather. That does give us less months to be available to the Ball State population so we really have to find ways to make our investment with Ball State Athletics work since we are not open year round and only about 8 months out of the year. And then there are the summer months where there is a pause on athletic events and students going home. That makes it feel a little more like 6 months. Our miniature golf course, Boulder Falls, and our frozen treats shop, The Frozen Boulder, are separate by name, but they are really underneath the same umbrella of our company and are connected on the same property. Again they feed off of each other for success. If we could incorporate both of them into the marketing and advertising partnership with Ball State, then we are willing to make the investment, and make this work. Let me know what you think, I know we have a deadline of August 16th approaching.

Sincerely

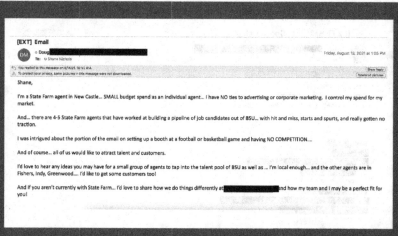

[EXT] Email

DM   o Doug ▮▮▮▮▮▮▮▮▮▮▮▮▮▮   Friday, August 13, 2021 at 1:05 PM
To: o Shane Nichols

You replied to this message on 8/14/21, 10:55 AM.
To protect your privacy, some pictures in this message were not downloaded.

Shane,

I'm a State Farm agent in New Castle... SMALL budget spend as an individual agent... I have NO ties to advertising or corporate marketing. I control my spend for my market.

And... there are 4-5 State Farm agents that have worked at building a pipeline of job candidates out of BSU... with hit and miss, starts and spurts, and really gotten no traction.

I was intrigued about the portion of the email on setting up a booth at a football or basketball game and having NO COMPETITION....

And of course... all of us would like to attract talent and customers.

I'd love to hear any ideas you may have for a small group of agents to tap into the talent pool of BSU as well as ... I'm local enough... and the other agents are in Fishers, Indy, Greenwood.... I'd like to get some customers too!

And if you aren't currently with State Farm... I'd love to share how we do things differently at ▮▮▮▮▮▮▮▮▮▮▮ and how my team and I may be a perfect fit for you!

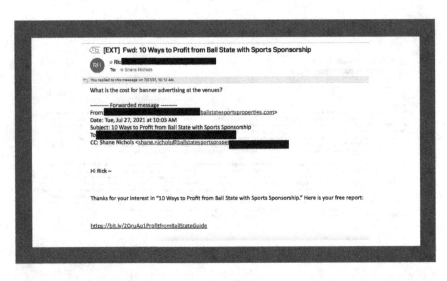

[EXT] Fwd: 10 Ways to Profit from Ball State with Sports Sponsorship

o Ric
To: o Shane Nichols

You replied to this message on 7/27/21, 10:12 AM.

What is the cost for banner advertising at the venues?

--------- Forwarded message ---------
From: ballstatesportsproperties.com>
Date: Tue, Jul 27, 2021 at 10:03 AM
Subject: 10 Ways to Profit from Ball State with Sports Sponsorship
To:
CC: Shane Nichols <shane.nichols@ballstatesprope

Hi Rick –

Thanks for your interest in "10 Ways to Profit from Ball State with Sports Sponsorship." Here is your free report:

https://bit.ly/2QruAg1ProfitfromBallStateGuide

[EXT] Ball State Sponsorship   Tracked To Dynamics 3

BS o Beth
To: o Shane Nichols   Monday, July 12, 2021 at 11:57 AM

You replied to this message on 7/12/21, 12:43 PM.   Show Reply

Good Morning,
I am interested in getting more information on sponsorship opportunities with Ball State , as well as the costs associated with the different options.
Thank you for your time.

--
Beth

Muncie, Indiana 47302

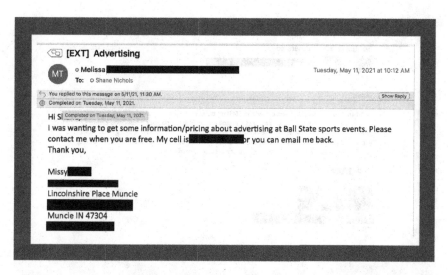

[EXT] Advertising

○ Melissa ▬▬▬▬▬▬▬▬▬   Tuesday, May 11, 2021 at 10:12 AM
To: ○ Shane Nichols

You replied to this message on 5/11/21, 11:30 AM.   [Show Reply]
Completed on Tuesday, May 11, 2021.

Hi S̶ Completed on Tuesday, May 11, 2021.
I was wanting to get some information/pricing about advertising at Ball State sports events. Please contact me when you are free. My cell is ▬▬▬▬▬ or you can email me back.
Thank you,

Missy ▬▬

Lincolnshire Place Muncie

Muncie IN 47304
▬▬▬▬▬

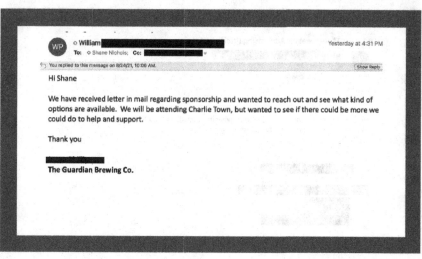

○ William ▬▬▬▬▬▬▬▬   Yesterday at 4:31 PM
To: ○ Shane Nichols;   Cc: ▬▬▬▬▬▬

You replied to this message on 8/24/21, 10:06 AM.   [Show Reply]

Hi Shane

We have received letter in mail regarding sponsorship and wanted to reach out and see what kind of options are available. We will be attending Charlie Town, but wanted to see if there could be more we could do to help and support.

Thank you

▬▬▬▬▬▬
The Guardian Brewing Co.

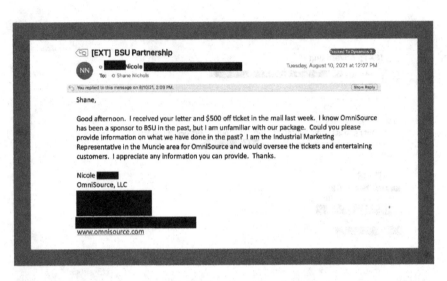

[EXT] BSU Partnership

NN | Nicole ▮ — To: Shane Nichols — Tuesday, August 10, 2021 at 12:07 PM — Tracked To Dynamics 3.

You replied to this message on 8/10/21, 2:09 PM. — Show Reply

Shane,

Good afternoon. I received your letter and $500 off ticket in the mail last week. I know OmniSource has been a sponsor to BSU in the past, but I am unfamiliar with our package. Could you please provide information on what we have done in the past? I am the Industrial Marketing Representative in the Muncie area for OmniSource and would oversee the tickets and entertaining customers. I appreciate any information you can provide. Thanks.

Nicole ▮
OmniSource, LLC

www.omnisource.com

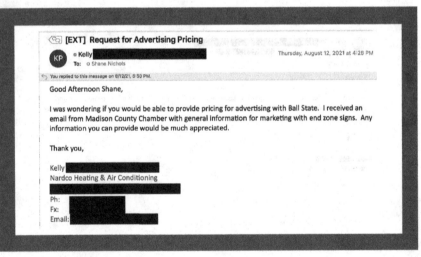

[EXT] Request for Advertising Pricing

KP | Kelly ▮ — To: Shane Nichols — Thursday, August 12, 2021 at 4:28 PM

You replied to this message on 8/12/21, 5:50 PM.

Good Afternoon Shane,

I was wondering if you would be able to provide pricing for advertising with Ball State. I received an email from Madison County Chamber with general information for marketing with end zone signs. Any information you can provide would be much appreciated.

Thank you,

Kelly ▮
Nardco Heating & Air Conditioning

Ph:
Fx:
Email:

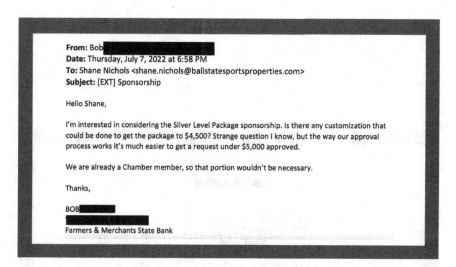

From: Bob ████████████████████
Date: Thursday, July 7, 2022 at 6:58 PM
To: Shane Nichols <shane.nichols@ballstatesportsproperties.com>
Subject: [EXT] Sponsorship

Hello Shane,

I'm interested in considering the Silver Level Package sponsorship. Is there any customization that could be done to get the package to $4,500? Strange question I know, but the way our approval process works it's much easier to get a request under $5,000 approved.

We are already a Chamber member, so that portion wouldn't be necessary.

Thanks,

BOB ████████████
████████████████████
Farmers & Merchants State Bank

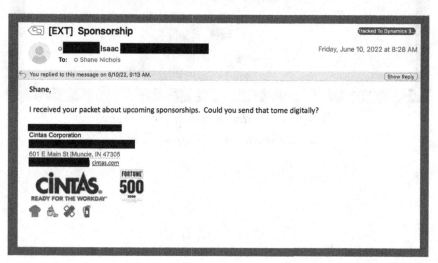

[EXT] Sponsorship

████████ Isaac ████████████████████   Friday, June 10, 2022 at 8:28 AM
To: ○ Shane Nichols

You replied to this message on 6/10/22, 9:13 AM.   [Show Reply]

Shane,

I received your packet about upcoming sponsorships. Could you send that tome digitally?

████████████████
Cintas Corporation

601 E Main St |Muncie, IN 47305
████████████████ cintas.com

CINTAS. FORTUNE 500
READY FOR THE WORKDAY

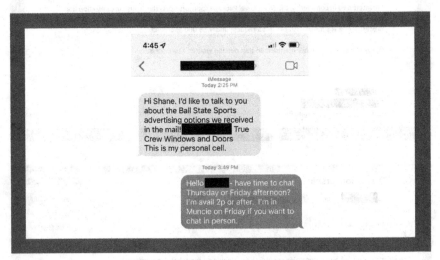

This person texted me out of the blue one day, turned into a $5,000 client

Subject: [EXT] Fwd: Social Media Is Hard

Mr. Nichols
I would appreciate it if you would remove me from your email and mailing lists. My experience with Ball State has not been the best, since Ball State has no interest in doing business with local business. Below is my experience.

Again thank you for letting us know about your service, but we advertise and support those that support us.

Kent

I got this response from a disgruntled alumni business owner who had bad experiences with Ball State's procurement process. This letter inspired a hook I used in my sales letters advising business owners that there are more riches in the Ball State Community - other than business owners, fans, etc. - rather than suffering through complicated and tedious RFP process of a state supported university.

[EXT] Sponsorships

AC ○ Anna████████████   Wednesday, July 6, 2022 at 10:44 AM

To: ○ Shane Nichols

You replied to this message on 7/6/22, 11:45 AM.   [Show Reply]

Hi Shane,

Wanted to reach out to see about your sponsorships and pricing. We do not have a large budget but wanted to see what you had to offer.

Thanks

Anna████████

PetermanBros.com • 677 Commerce Pkwy W Dr • Greenwood, IN 46143

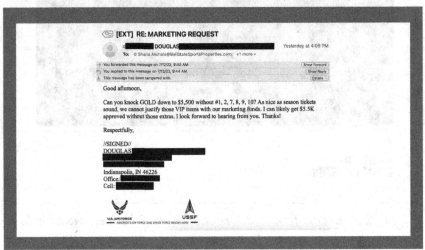

[EXT] RE: MARKETING REQUEST

○████████ DOUGLAS████████   Yesterday at 4:09 PM

To: ○ Shane.Nichols@BallStateSportsProperties.com; +1 more ∨

You forwarded this message on 7/12/22, 9:40 AM.   [Show Forward]
You replied to this message on 7/12/22, 9:44 AM.   [Show Reply]
This message has been tampered with.   [Details]

Good afternoon,

Can you knock GOLD down to $5,500 without #1, 2, 7, 8, 9, 10? As nice as season tickets sound, we cannot justify those VIP items with our marketing funds. I can likely get $5.5K approved without those extras. I look forward to hearing from you. Thanks!

Respectfully,

//SIGNED//
DOUGLAS████████

Indianapolis, IN 46226
Office:████████
Cell:████████

U.S. AIR FORCE   USSF
AMERICA'S AIR FORCE AND SPACE FORCE BEGINS HERE

Above and below are two responses I received to a direct mail campaign that marketed some specific sponsorship packages. Without any additional effort on my part these two sponsors emailed me with their orders totaling $12,500 in sponsorship revenue!

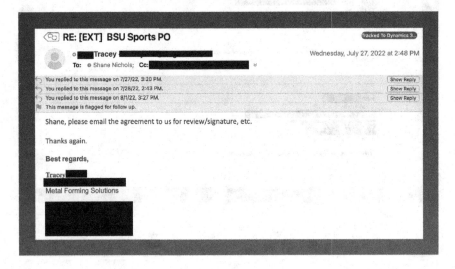

This response was from a Fed Ex. I sent this person's boss — the CEO of a hospital multiple letters. It was only after sending the Fed Ex did, they finally respond.

This email came to me from a person who works for the state of Indiana and has a sizable budget for marketing, meaning he is the target of dozens of salespeople, every day. He received 3 letters, a voicemail, and then the day he accepted my LinkedIn request – my 3rd type of media vying for his attention, he sent me this email. The perfect result to a campaign is having the prospect responding and reaching out to me, putting me in a perfect position to close.

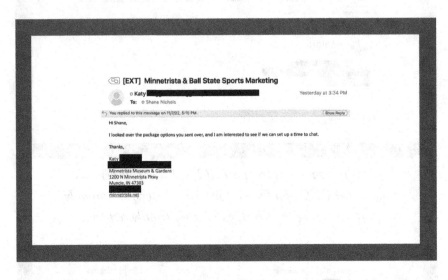

[EXT] **Minnetrista & Ball State Sports Marketing**

○ Katy ██████████████████████   Yesterday at 3:34 PM
To: ○ Shane Nichols

↩ You replied to this message on 11/7/22, 5:16 PM.   [Show Reply]

Hi Shane,

I looked over the package options you sent over, and I am interested to see if we can set up a time to chat.

Thanks,

Katy ████████
Minnetrista Museum & Gardens
1200 N Minnetrista Pkwy
Muncie, IN 47303
██████
minnetrista.net

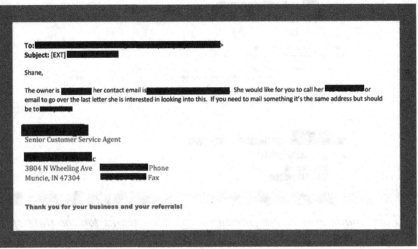

To: ████████████████████████████████████▶
Subject: [EXT] ████████████

Shane,

The owner is ████████ her contact email is ████████████████████. She would like for you to call her ████████████ or email to go over the last letter she is interested in looking into this. If you need to mail something it's the same address but should be to ████████

████████████
Senior Customer Service Agent

████████████c
3804 N Wheeling Ave   ████████ Phone
Muncie, IN 47304   ████████ Fax

Thank you for your business and your referrals!

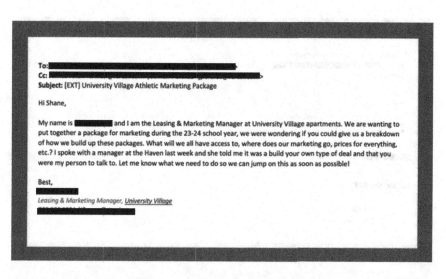

To: ██
Cc: ██
Subject: [EXT] University Village Athletic Marketing Package

Hi Shane,

My name is ████████████ and I am the Leasing & Marketing Manager at University Village apartments. We are wanting to put together a package for marketing during the 23-24 school year, we were wondering if you could give us a breakdown of how we build up these packages. What will we all have access to, where does our marketing go, prices for everything, etc.? I spoke with a manager at the Haven last week and she told me it was a build your own type of deal and that you were my person to talk to. Let me know what we need to do so we can jump on this as soon as possible!

Best,
████████████
Leasing & Marketing Manager, University Village
████████████████

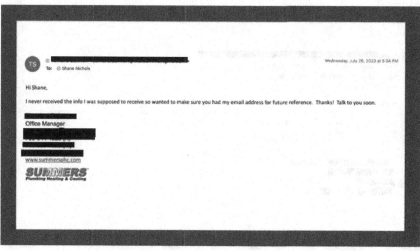

████████████████████████████████
To: Shane Nichols   Wednesday, July 26, 2023 at 6:04 PM

Hi Shane,

I never received the info I was supposed to receive so wanted to make sure you had my email address for future reference. Thanks! Talk to you soon.

████████████
Office Manager
████████████
████████████
www.summersphc.com

SUMMERS
Plumbing Heating & Cooling

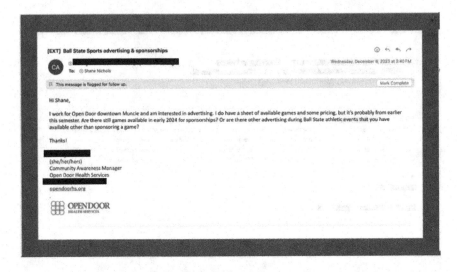

[EXT] Ball State Sports advertising & sponsorships

To: Shane Nichols

Wednesday, December 8, 2023 at 3:40 PM

This message is flagged for follow up.

Mark Complete

Hi Shane,

I work for Open Door downtown Muncie and am interested in advertising. I do have a sheet of available games and some pricing, but it's probably from earlier this semester. Are there still games available in early 2024 for sponsorships? Or are there other advertising during Ball State athletic events that you have available other than sponsoring a game?

Thanks!

(she/her/hers)
Community Awareness Manager
Open Door Health Services

opendoorhs.org

OPEN DOOR
HEALTH SERVICES

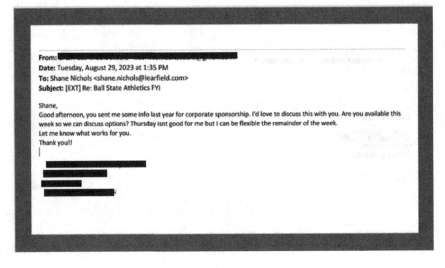

From:

Date: Tuesday, August 29, 2023 at 1:35 PM
To: Shane Nichols <shane.nichols@learfield.com>
Subject: [EXT] Re: Ball State Athletics FYI

Shane,
Good afternoon, you sent me some info last year for corporate sponsorship. I'd love to discuss this with you. Are you available this week so we can discuss options? Thursday isnt good for me but I can be flexible the remainder of the week.
Let me know what works for you.
Thank you!!

Shane,

I received your packet in the mail related to the executive membership sponsor request and wanted to follow up with you on developing a specific package and what different price points look like as far as what benefits would be at each tier. This isn't something we have money set aside for in this year's budget, but we are curious to learn more.

Thanks,

WURSTER CONSTRUCTION — Built for Life

ABC STEP — Associated Builders and Contractors — 2023 STEP Diamond

[EXT] 5k:

To: Shane Nichols

Yesterday at 2:02 PM

This message is flagged for follow up.

Mark Complete

Shane , just opened your envelope. Have some questions. I played Football at BSU many years ago and i am more intgerested in the football games etc. It states: "Just let us know when you'd like to come and enjoy VIP parking and VIP hospitality access to all Men's and Women's conference BASKETBALL games at Worthen Arena, where you can enjoy snacks. soda ands a pre-game speech from our coach.

MY QUESTION IS I AM MORE INTERESTED IN FOOTBALL NOT BASKETBALL FOR THIS VIP EXPERIENCE. HELP!!

Is these UNLIMITED games to attend for football and Basketball etc??

Regards,

[EXT] From New Destination Weddings re: Executive Member Club

  Yesterday at 12:03 PM

To: Shane Nichols

ⓘ Completed on Monday, July 22, 2024.

Hello Shane,

Your letter sounds interesting, but I'm not exactly certain where my type of business would fit into your type of advertising.

I am a Wedding Officiant, a person who marries two people. I perform everything from small elopements to elaborate, custom-written ceremonies. I've been in business for almost 20 years and have married approximately a thousand couples. That's not counting the commitment ceremonies, vow renewals, and Wiccan/pagan and Viking ceremonies. I also do themed ceremonies, such as medieval, Viking, renaissance, Star Trek, Star Wars, Dr. Who...if you can name it, I can probably do it.

[EXT] Chateau Kitchens - Executive Member

  Wednesday, July 10, 2024 at 7:47 AM

To: Shane Nichols

Shane,

I received your letter in the mail. Count Chateau Kitchens & Home Remodeling in.

Let me know what the next steps are.

Thank you,

Owner
Chateau Kitchens & Home Remodeling

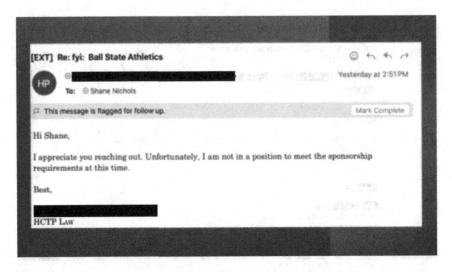

[EXT] Re: fyi: Ball State Athletics

HP   Yesterday at 2:51 PM

To: Shane Nichols

This message is flagged for follow up.   Mark Complete

Hi Shane,

I appreciate you reaching out. Unfortunately, I am not in a position to meet the sponsorship requirements at this time.

Best,

HCTP LAW

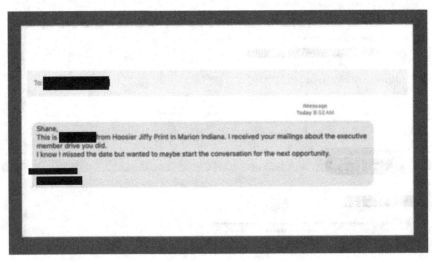

To:

iMessage
Today 8:52 AM

Shane,
This is _____ from Hoosier Jiffy Print in Marion Indiana. I received your mailings about the executive member drive you did.
I know I missed the date but wanted to maybe start the conversation for the next opportunity.

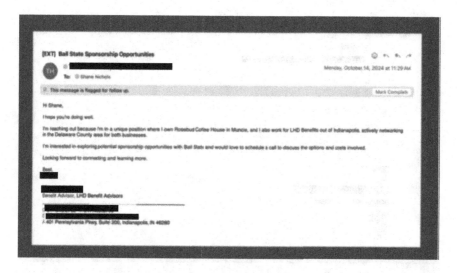

[EXT] Ball State Sponsorship Opportunities

To: Shane Nichols

Monday, October 14, 2024 at 11:29 AM

This message is flagged for follow up.

Mark Complete

Hi Shane,

I hope you're doing well.

I'm reaching out because I'm in a unique position where I own Rosebud Coffee House in Muncie, and I also work for LHD Benefits out of Indianapolis, actively networking in the Delaware County area for both businesses.

I'm interested in exploring potential sponsorship opportunities with Ball State and would love to schedule a call to discuss the options and costs involved.

Looking forward to connecting and learning more.

Best,

Benefit Advisor, LHD Benefit Advisors

401 Pennsylvania Pkwy, Suite 200, Indianapolis, IN 46280

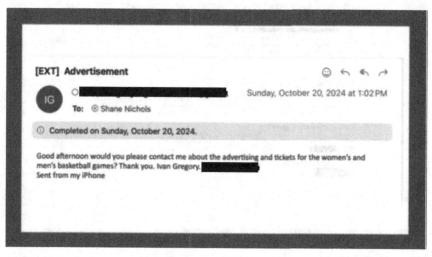

[EXT] Advertisement

To: Shane Nichols

Sunday, October 20, 2024 at 1:02 PM

Completed on Sunday, October 20, 2024.

Good afternoon would you please contact me about the advertising and tickets for the women's and men's basketball games? Thank you. Ivan Gregory.
Sent from my iPhone

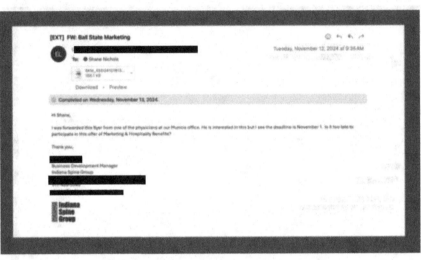

Resources

The books that helped me to learn how to generate leads:

- *No B.S. Direct Marketing: The Ultimate No Holds Barred Kick Butt Take No Prisoners Direct Marketing for Non-Direct Marketing Businesses, No B.S. Sales Success In the New Economy, The Ultimate Sales Letter, Magnetic Marketing, Renegade Millionaire: 7 Secrets to Extreme Wealth, Autonomy, And Entrepreneurial Success, No B.S. Guide to Succeeding in Business by Breaking All the Rules, Maximum Referrals & Customer Retention The Ultimate No Holds Barred Plan To Securing New Customers and Maximum Profits, Grassroots Marketing The Ultimate Guide to Growing Sales and Profits of Local Small Businesses* by Dan S. Kennedy
- *Getting Everything You Can Out of All You've Got: 21 Ways You Can Out-Think, Out-Perform, and Out-Earn the Competition 21 Ways You Can Out-Think, Out-Perform, and Out-Earn the Competition* by Jay Abraham

- *The Ultimate Sales Machine* by Chet Holmes
- *Predictable Revenue: Turn Your Business into a Sales Machine with the $100M Best Practices of Salesforce.com* by Aaron Ross, Tyler & Marylou Pebblestorm
- *The Education of Millionaires: Everything You Won't Learn in College About How to Be Successful* by Michael Ellsberg
- *The 80/20 Principle: The Secret to Achieving More with Less* by Richard Koch
- *Winning Through Intimidation* by Robert Ringer
- *How To Get a Meeting with Anyone* by Stu Heinecke
- *Sell Like Crazy* by Sabri Suby
- *Traffic Secrets, Expert Secrets, Dot Com Secrets* by Russell Brunson
- *The War of Art* by Steven Pressfield
- *Tested Advertising Methods & How to Make Your Advertising Make You Money* by John Caples
- *How to Make Maximum Money in Minimum Time, The Boron Letters* by Gary Halbert
- *Ogilvy on Advertising* by David Ogilvy
- *Advertising Secrets of the Written Word: The Ultimate Resource on How to Write Powerful Advertising Copy from One of America's Top Copywriters and Mail Order Entrepreneurs* by Joseph Sugarman
- *Reason Why Advertising* by John E Kennedy
- *My Life in Advertising, Scientific Advertising* by Claude C Hopkins
- *Reality in Advertising* by Rosser Reeves
- *Outrageous Advertising That's Outrageously Successful: Created for 99% of Small Business Owners*

Who Are Dissatisfied with the Results They Get by Bill Glazer and Dan S. Kennedy

- *Effective Frequency: The Relationship Between Frequency and Advertising Effectiveness* by Michael Naples
- *Handbook of Direct Mail: The Dialogue Method of Direct Communication* by Siegfried Vogele
- *The Greatest Direct Mail Sales Letters of All Time: Why They Succeed, How They're Created, How You Can Create Great Sales Letters, too!* By Hodgson, Richard S.
- *The Golden Mailbox* by Ted Nicholas
- *The Lazy Man's Way to Riches* by Joe Carbo
- *Kick Ass Copywriting Secrets of a Marketing Rebel* by John Carlton

About the Author

Shane Nichols started his professional career in college selling advertising for the campus newspaper. He quickly emerged as a sales leader, getting promoted to sales manager. And this has been the story throughout his career, transitioning from newspaper to magazines, from magazines to radio, from radio to television, from television to sports sponsorship, Shane is a recognized leader and award-winning seller wherever he goes.

Shane published his first book, *The Intelligent Advertiser: The Definitive Guide to Finding Value in Broadcast Media,* in 2018. And *The 7 Habits of Highly Effective Advertisers*, was published in the fall of 2020. Both are available on Amazon.

How I Can Help

Would you like some help with your own B2B or B2C lead generation marketing efforts, I'm happy to provide the following services.

1. **CONSULTING:** Hire me to advise on your new business development strategy.
2. **COACHING:** Hire me to coach you on your journey of implementing your own inbound and outbound lead generation strategy.
3. **SPEAKING:** Hire me to speak at your event and teach advanced prospecting strategy and tactics.
4. **PROJECTS:** Hire me to write/develop a unique selling point, selling hooks and angles, sales letters and more. Or, let me take all the work off your plate by creating an entire inbound and outbound lead generation system, all done for you.

Email is the best way to reach me:
michaelshanenichols@gmail.com

Printed in the United States
by Baker & Taylor Publisher Services